P9-CFZ-228

SIGNS OF WONDER

SIGNS
OF
WONDER

The
Phenomenon
of Convergence
in Modern
Liturgical and
Charismatic
Churches

ROBERT WEBBER

ABBOTT
MARTYN
A DIVISION OF
STAR SONG PUBLISHING GROUP
NASHVILLE, TENNESSEE

Star Song Publishing Group, a division of Jubilee Communications, Inc.
2325 Crestmoor, Nashville, Tennessee 37215.
Printed in the United States of America.

First Printing, March 1992

Library of Congress Cataloging-in-Publication Data

Webber, Robert.
    Signs of wonder : the phenomenon of convergence in modern
liturgical and charismatic churches / by Robert Webber.
      p. cm.
    Includes bibliographical references.
    ISBN 1-56233-000-4 : $12.95
    1. Public worship. 2. Liturgical churches. 3. Pentecostalism.
I. Title.
BV15.W38   1992
264—dc20   91-35891
                                                 CIP

1 2 3 4 5 6 7 8 9 10 — 96 95 94 93 92

Acknowledgments

THE WRITING OF A BOOK is always dependent on a number of different people. This book could not have been written without my editors, Matthew Price and Lisa Guest, to whom I owe much for their encouragement, critiques, and line editing. I also wish to thank the many churches and pastors who have influenced my thought and whose work in ministry inspired the contents of this book. A special word of thanks to the following ministers and churches who cooperated with the writing of this book: Rev. Scott Bauer, The Church on the Way, Van Nuys, California; Rev. Randall Davey, Overland Park Nazarene Church, Overland Park, Kansas; Rev. Joe Horness, Willow Creek Community Church, South Barrington, Illinois; Rev. Ron Jackson, St. Bartholomew's Episcopal Church, Nashville, Tennessee; Rev. Richard Lobs, St. Mark's Episcopal Church, Geneva, Illinois; Rev. Doug Mills, Christ Covenant Church, Gatlinburg, Tennessee; Cathleen Morris, Celebration Community, Aliquippa, Pennsylvania; Rev. Ben Patterson, Irvine Presbyterian Church, Irvine, California, and now The Presbyterian Church at New Providence, New Providence, New Jersey; Rev. Steven Shoemaker, Crescent Hill Baptist Church, Louisville, Kentucky; Rev. Chuck Smith, Jr., Calvary Chapel, Capistrano Beach, California; Rev. Robert Till, Midway Baptist Church, Dallas, Texas; and Rev. Mark Weinart, Willow Creek Community Church, South Barrington, Illinois. And finally a special word of thanks to my secretary, Mary Lou McCurdy, who has faithfully typed and retyped this work.

100555

Contents

Introduction

FOR MORE THAN TEN YEARS I have been traveling among Christians of nearly every denomination and talking with them about worship. For this reason I feel I have some sense of what is happening among contemporary churches.

Two matters keep emerging and they come from what one may think to be the opposite ends of the kingdom.

The one is interest in liturgical renewal.

The other is interest in the charismatic movement.

I don't mean to suggest all people are equally interested in these two movements. Indeed there are those who see red when the word liturgical is used and those who see the devil in the charismatic movement.

These are extremes. But they are there.

Those who are interested in the liturgical movement are not necessarily ready to become liturgical. What they are interested in is the rich tradition, the heritage, the beauty, the order, the content, and substance of prayer book worship.

Those who are interested in the charismatic movement are not necessarily ready to join a charismatic church or adopt all of its practices.

What grabs their attention is the freedom, the spontaneity, the joy, the warmth, and the sense of community felt among charismatics.

What's happening as a result of these interests is a borrowing of traditions. I have been in many liturgical churches that borrow the charismatic choruses and styles and integrate more freedom into their structure.

Likewise, I have been in many charismatic churches that are borrowing from the liturgical tradition. I cannot tell you how many charismatics own and draw from the Book of Common Prayer, but I know it's more than a smattering of people here and there. And charismatics are saying publicly they want more content, more substance to their worship.

I have also seen in many churches that are neither liturgical nor charismatic who, because of their commitment to worship renewal, are borrowing from both liturgical and charismatic traditions.

Because of this mutual borrowing from the liturgical and charismatic churches, I see a convergence of worship traditions taking place.

Many years ago Richard Lovelace, professor of spirituality at Gordon-Conwell Theological Seminary, said, "Lets face it, Bob, our young people are going toward artistry or ecstasy."

I believe he was right and that his utterance is even more true today.

And furthermore, I believe what is happening worldwide in worship is a convergence of the traditions—a convergence that is resulting in the birth of a style of worship that is rooted in the Scriptures, aware of the developments in history, and with a passion for the contemporary.

This is a book about that convergence, a phenomenon which, I believe, is a sign of wonder.

Robert Webber
Wheaton, Illinois
Pentecost 1991

SECTION I

◇

What's Happening in Worshiping Churches?

◇

1

$\diamond$

Worship Styles in Dialogue with Each Other

Worshiping churches respect their own tradition, are in dialogue with the worship traditions of other churches, and draw from the church's worship practices throughout history.

MY MOST MEMORABLE ENCOUNTER with a style of worship different from my own occurred at a weekend retreat more than twenty years ago. I had joined a praise and prayer group while doing graduate work at Concordia Theological Seminary in St. Louis. The group consisted of Catholics, Lutherans, Presbyterians, and evangelicals who met monthly to read and discuss Scripture, to pray together, to talk, and to just have fun. When the time came for many of us to graduate and move on to new places, we decided to bring our two-year fellowship to an end with a weekend retreat at a local Catholic conference center. It was there that we faced an issue we had never even discussed. Could we take Communion together? Could a Catholic priest give the bread and wine to an evangelical? Could an evangelical receive the bread and wine from a Catholic priest?

We were all sitting on the lawn of the monastery near the chapel. The monastery stood on a hill overlooking the rich Missouri farmland, and the smell of fresh spring grass was in the air. I heard the priest say, "We are going to conclude our retreat with a liturgy in the chapel. You are, of course, all welcome to come, but I don't know what to say to you about the bread and wine. As a rule, we Catholics only allow other Catholics to receive the body and blood of the Lord. But I have agonized over this separation of our churches, as I know you have."

He paused and continued, "I have decided to break with Catholic tradition and offer you the bread and wine. Why? Because it is my experience that all of you are true Christians devoted to our Lord. But I cannot tell any of you what to do. You may not feel comfortable receiving the bread and wine. You must make that decision for yourself. If you don't come to receive, your decision will be respected, and if you do come, you will be welcomed."

As I thought about this invitation, I looked down the dirt road that led to the paved highway. The road was lined on both sides with tall, stately trees. Their limbs stretched out, touching each other over the driveway and creating a green, leafy canopy. I then looked around at the plain, sparkling white buildings silhouetted against the blue sky, spotted by a few rolling clouds and a bright, hospitable sun. My eyes settled on the small chapel. I glanced at the cross on the roof, the small stained-glass windows, and the heavy oak door.

I then lifted my face toward the sun and felt its warmth. Closing my eyes, I allowed my life in the church to pass before me. My prejudices rose up within me: *"What are you doing here? You've never worshiped in a Catholic setting, let alone received the bread and wine from a Catholic priest!"* Then I considered the spiritually rich times I'd shared with these people for two years. I heard again my Catholic friends speak of their love for Christ, pray with fervency, and express a real desire to know the Scriptures and live by its authority. Those memories said, *"Go ahead. After all, there is only one Lord, one church, one faith, one baptism, one Holy Communion."*

In that moment, God broke through the walls I had allowed to separate me from my brothers and sisters of different denominations. I'm convinced that the prejudices we hold and the walls we build between ourselves and other communities of Christians actually block our experience of God's presence in our lives. Our biases cut us off from the spiritual communion of the fullness of the body of Christ. God dwells in his church, and to reject a part of God's church is to reject him. Furthermore, rejecting a part of God's church keeps us from experiencing what the creed calls "the communion of the Saints." When God broke down my walls, he brought me into a richer fellowship with the body of Christ throughout the world.

When I stepped into the small, inviting chapel, I also stepped into my first experience with the liturgical. I wasn't accustomed to the worship environment—to the large table balancing the pulpit, to burning candles, to a worship leader dressed in vestments, to a guitar and folk songs mixed with an ancient chant and a classic hymn. I wasn't familiar with the kind of participation demanded of me—the dialogue, acclamation, and three Scripture readings punctuated by psalms, the bidding prayers, the passing of the peace, the personal touch of the priest calling me by name as he gave me the bread and wine, and the praise and celebration expressed in the Communion song. You might say I was surprised by joy! I found myself ministering to God in praise, and God in turn was ministering to me. I had never had an experience like that in my life. In that Catholic chapel, a new worship experience had bumped up against an old prejudice of mine, and a new attitude was born. I had taken into myself the experience of another tradition, I had been in dialogue with another worship tradition, and I was surely the richer for it.

Prejudice, Dialogue, and Historical Consciousness

In this opportunity to worship with believers from other denominations and different styles of worship, I was forced to face my own prejudice. I had specific convictions about worship and definite ideas about those forms of worship that varied from my tastes and standards. But this time I took off the blinders of my preconceived ideas. I let myself enter into dialogue with a form of worship I had never experienced and therefore never fully understood. As I engaged in this dialogue, I found myself developing a new awareness of the church throughout history.

These images of prejudice, dialogue, and historical consciousness—which, with the help of philosopher Hans-Georg Gadamer, I'll soon better define—are important because they point to what is happening in worshiping churches today. Each church has a prejudice—be it liturgical, traditional Protestant, creative, or praise tradition worship—that biases it against other worship traditions. But lately congregations are talking with one another. Believers are listening to and learning from each other's experiences. At the same time, they are entering into dialogue with the historical tradition of the church as a whole. Resulting from this new relationship is a convergence of worship traditions. A spirit of oneness and openness is bringing the church together in a new experience of worship. This is not an isolated phenomenon found here or there, but a movement found to one degree or another in all worshiping churches, in all churches that are experiencing the transforming power of God.

Allow me to illustrate this convergence and new openness by telling a little more about my own experience with prejudice, my dialogue with various worship traditions, and my movement toward an historical consciousness of the church. I do so not to present my own experience as a standard, but to illustrate what is happening for many people in the church throughout the world.

Prejudice

I am a graduate of four distinctly conservative institutions—Bob Jones University, Reformed Episcopal Seminary, Covenant Theological Seminary, and Concordia Theological Seminary. I am also a professor of theology at Wheaton College and Graduate School, an evangelical institution known for its conservative point of view.

As you might expect, I have been decidedly influenced by my experiences at these various institutions and the church groups they represent. And, as the philosopher Hans-Georg Gadamer would say, I carry around within me these influences as well as influences from home and from life in general. Gadamer calls these experiences "prejudices." I have, you might say, a conditioning within me that I cannot completely overcome; I hold prejudices from such diverse sources as fundamentalism, Calvinism, Lutheranism, and evangelicalism. These points of view influence the way I think about the Christian faith and the way I worship.

All of us—and our churches—have dispositions of this sort. It's not that we are intentionally prejudiced. Instead, the environments in which we were raised and in which we have worshiped build within us convictions that we may not even be able to identify.

For example, the nonliturgical background of my early years naturally made me skeptical about both the liturgical and charismatic traditions of worship. I was suspicious of anyone who did not believe or practice the Christian faith as I did. And I was dead certain that I was right and they were wrong.

These prejudices became ingrained during my years at home and my formative years in college. I can point to an incident when I was twelve years old that surely built prejudice within me. The story goes like this: A Reformed couple came to our Baptist parsonage to visit with my parents. As they were deeply engaged in conversation about some religious matter—the favorite topic in my home—the male visitor lighted a cigarette right there in our living room. I was shocked. How could someone talk about religion and smoke at the same time?

As soon as our guests left, I quickly made my way to my mother's side. "Mother, I thought those people were Christians. How can somebody smoke and be a Christian?" My mother's answer was classic: "Well, Robert, they are Reformed. And Reformed people, though they are Christian, have funny ideas and do worldly things. But we are Baptists, the best of the Christian groups. We don't have funny ideas and we aren't worldly." Right then and there, in that young and impressionable mind, a prejudice was set in place.

I had similar experiences in college. I can, for example, distinctly remember the founder of the college cupping his hands over his mouth in chapel and crying, "Do you want to know where a man stands with God?" Obviously anyone who is spiritually sensitive wants to know how to determine a person's standing with God. I leaned forward, anxiously awaiting his answer. "You only have to ask that person one question," he continued. Then, after a moment's pause, came the confident, dogmatic assertion, "Ask him, 'What do you think of this university?'"

Now I was aware of how people felt about that university. Some thought the school was reactionary, racist, legalistic, dogmatic, and arrogant. "What about those people?" I thought. "Is God angry with them? Have they really fallen away from the truth?" As I recalled other assertions I'd heard proclaimed at the college, I found myself asking, "Is everybody in the World Council of Churches an apostate renegade seeking to destroy the true church? Are all liturgical people really ritualists, servants of a dead orthodoxy given to vain repetition? Is the charismatic movement really of the devil?" With all of these questions, I was dealing with prejudices that had long ago been planted in my mind like seeds placed in the rich, dark soil of a spring garden.

Dialogue

Instead of nurturing those seeds of prejudice, I chose to journey beyond the confines of my fundamentalist education into an Episcopal seminary, then a Presbyterian seminary, and finally a Lutheran school.

In these schools and through the experiences I had there, I began to do what philosopher Gadamer calls "dialogue." Everyone knows what that common word means. "Dialogue" means to interact with, to exchange ideas—and in these schools I entered into dialogue about my prejudices. I met people who had grown up with their own conditioning and who held points of view very different from my own. I interfaced with Calvinists and Arminians, with liturgical people and charismatics. It was prejudice against prejudice, tradition against tradition, experience against experience. But what might have been confrontation became dialogue.

I can remember my first encounter with the charismatic tradition, an experience that again goes back to my days in college. A group of students had been gathering on a regular basis, imploring God in prayer to give them a fresh experience of the Holy Spirit. And God did just that. They experienced a manifestation of the Spirit which brought them a new freedom in prayer and worship. And, as their numbers grew, they invited me to join with them. I can still remember how we were all gathered on our knees in a classroom, praying out loud. It was fervent and passionate prayer, prayer that begged and implored and knocked on the door, prayer that ultimately broke out in glossolalia.

Frankly, I was very afraid of what I was hearing. It seemed strange and unnecessary. I only went once. My fear of emotionalism and fanaticism was a long-held prejudice within me. I was not yet ready to enter into dialogue with the charismatic tradition.

It was many years later when I began to dialogue with the charismatic or what I now prefer to call "praise and worship tradition." At the time, I was already teaching at Wheaton College. Through various contacts, I came to know Bob Walker, editor of *Christian Life* magazine and owner of the publishing firm Creation House. A young and growing company, Creation House asked me if I would serve as its editor-in-chief on a part-time basis. This position put me in touch with charismatics and the praise and worship tradition. I soon discovered that, although there were some people on the extreme, at the core of this tradition were people who had had a real and vital experience with the Holy Spirit and who enjoyed a freedom in their worship that I in my evangelical tradition did not experience.

During this time, I visited a young but growing Assembly of God congregation in Naperville, a church now well-known for its ministry in the Chicago area. The building that housed Calvary Church was a plain, two-story structure with Sunday school space on the first floor and worship space upstairs. Although rather small, the place teemed with bustling, cheery people who greeted me warmly. I was made to feel at home by these people who were strangers to me not only by birth, but also by their worship tradition.

The service itself was quite disarming. It began with the song "There's a Sweet, Sweet Spirit in This Place." As the music minister continued to lead the various choruses and hymns, I experienced the reality of the comment I had heard from nearly every praise and worship tradition person I had met: God inhabits the praise of his people. It really did seem as though the glory of God came upon that congregation as they became lost in praise and wonder. Although not really good at letting myself go because of my built-in prejudices, I found that as I increasingly lost myself in praise and worship and focused on the majesty and holiness of God, earth grew strangely dim in the light of his wonder and praise.

In this and other experiences with praise and worship tradition worship, I realized I was dialoguing with another prejudice. Furthermore, I was beginning to integrate my praise tradition worship experience into the sum total of my spiritual life. As a result of these varied experiences, I found myself becoming a new person, and I was decidedly richer for it.

Historical Consciousness

According to philosopher Gadamer, we not only hold within us prejudices from our background—which in dialogue with another perspective may cause growth—but we are also people of an historical consciousness which we cannot escape. We may, of course, deny our historical belongingness and suppress it, but it is still there. This insight provides yet another important key to what is happening in the church and in worship today: dialogue with historical consciousness.

The truth is that we Americans are a-historical. Most of us know very little about history and probably care even less. What we are interested in is the now, the moment, the existential experience. Unfortunately, most churches in this country have the same mentality. This is especially true of conservative Protestant churches. We are a succession of breakaways with a constant history of starting over again without attention to or respect for our parental history. Unfortunately, when it comes to worship, there is a terrible price to pay for this attitude. When we cut ourselves off from the rich treasury of resources and from the collective spirituality of God's people

throughout the ages, we diminish our vision of God. We isolate ourselves from what God would do in the world through us, his
church.

I was indifferent to the history of the church and to the history
of worship until I went to graduate school. I can still vividly remember a course I took on the Apostolic Fathers (leaders of the church
between A.D. 100–150). I went into that class with a definite prejudice against them. I was convinced—not on the basis of intelligent
investigation, but through unfounded rumor and hearsay—that the
church became apostate by the end of the first century and that
nothing of any spiritual value happened in the church until Martin
Luther tacked his ninety-five theses on the door of the Wittenberg
church. I now cringe to think I ever thought or believed anything
so unintelligent and so obviously prejudicial, but I did. What a surprise it was for me to discover the heart and passion of these Fathers
of the church, and how humiliating it is for me now, more than
twenty years later, to acknowledge that I have yet to plumb the
depths of these lovers of God and framers of our faith.

But I am not alone in this discovery of my Christian roots. I
constantly meet church leaders and students who are discovering a
sense of belonging to the historical Christian church and the worldwide Christian church of today. There is a new awareness of our
Christian ancestors and of what we can learn from them. As we reclaim the past for the present, the God who breaks into history
breaks into our lives.

I am convinced that the more we dialogue with the rich heritage of worship in the church, the richer we will be. We need to con-
verse with the worship of the Orthodox, Catholic, Lutheran,
Anglican, Reformed, Anabaptist, Quaker, Methodist, Pentecostal,
charismatic, and evangelical traditions. Each of these has something
to offer the others, and all of them together—plus traditions I have
not named—represent the fullness of the church and the variety of
gifts given to the church by the Holy Spirit.

I have found that the churches growing through worship are
dialoguing with the biblical and early church tradition of worship.
What the Holy Spirit gave to the church in its early years is foun-
dational and consequently of the utmost importance for the building
up of our worship today. As with spiritual renewals of the past, the
worship renewal of the church today is due largely to the rediscovery of the insights of the framers of our faith and the resources they

have left us. The same Fathers who hammered out the authority of Scripture, wrote the great creeds, developed the disciplines of spirituality, and clarified the ethics of the church are the Fathers through whom the Spirit still delivers the keys to our understanding and practice of worship. We have much to gain by dialoguing with the tradition of early Christian worship.

Conclusion

As you read these pages, you may ask: Why have you taken us down this route? Why have you told personal stories about prejudice, about dialogue, and about historical consciousness?

My answer is simple: My experience seems to be a microcosm of what is happening in people's lives and in churches all over the world—and apparently happening without any connections. God seems to be doing a new work in our time, a work of breaking down prejudices, bringing his people together, and uniting us to the common history of the church. And the place where this is happening is in worship—in a worship that crosses traditions, joins them into one seamless robe, and allows the people of these various traditions to worship not as separate entities, but as one church. Of course there are those who still hold on to their prejudices. Of course there are those who refuse to enter into dialogue with other traditions. Of course there are those who ignore the history of God's common family. But their number is smaller than it was a year ago.

Furthermore, there is a growing consensus that, in the future, Christian worship will be characterized by the blending of the traditional and the contemporary into a vital experience of worship and praise. This book seeks to describe and encourage this process which is taking place in churches around the world. The convergence of worship traditions will break down the barriers we have built against other Christians. Also, through renewed worship, God is breaking through a perceived absence in our lives to create an exciting sense of his presence in the worship services of his people.

Bibliography

For a better understanding of the philosophical idea of prejudice, dialogue, and historical consciousness, read Hans-Georg Gadamer, *Philosophical Hermeneutics* (Berkeley: University of California Press, 1976). The best interpretation of Gadamer's work is found in Richard E. Palmer, *Hermeneutics* (Evanston: Northwestern University Press, 1969).

To understand the different traditions of worship, I recommend J. G. Davies (ed.), *The New Westminster Dictionary of Liturgy and Worship* (Louisville: Westminster John Knox Press, 1986). In this dictionary, you will find a sympathetic description of each major tradition of Christian worship.

For a more detailed description of the Orthodox tradition, I suggest Hans-Joachim Schulz, *The Byzantine Liturgy* (New York: Pueblo, 1986). This book gives a thorough interpretation of the John Chrysostom Liturgy (A.D. 380) and thus provides rich insight not only into the Orthodox tradition of worship, but also into the theological roots of Orthodox worship in the Patristic period. Herman Wegman, *Christian Worship in East and West* (New York: Pueblo, 1985), has written an excellent history of worship through the medieval period in which both Catholic and Orthodox worship are compared in their historical and cultural settings. An excellent theology of Catholic worship is set forth in Edward J. Kilmartin, S.J., *Christian Liturgy* (Kansas City: Sheed and Ward, 1988). Robert Taft, S.J., tackles problems in both Orthodox and Catholic worship in *Beyond East and West: Problems in Liturgical Understanding* (Washington: The Pastoral Press, 1984). This book is not only a scholarly masterpiece; it is eminently pastoral. His main argument is that one cannot fully understand the theology and embrace the practices of worship without a good grasp of the historical issues.

Much less material has been published to explain the roots of Protestant worship. The best book available is James F. White, *Protestant Worship: Tradition in Transition* (Louisville: Westminster John Knox Press, 1989). A very helpful book on early American Protestant worship is Doug Adams, *Meeting House to Camp Meeting: Toward a History of American Free Church Worship from 1620 to 1835* (Austin: The Shearing Company, 1981). Finally, Oliphant Hughes Old has written a scholarly book tracing the roots of Protestant worship back to the Patristic era. This work, *The Patristic Roots of Reformed Worship* (Zurich: Theologischer Verlag Zurich, 1975), is probably available only in seminary libraries.

Charismatic or praise and worship tradition worship is best set forth by Jack W. Hayford, *Worship His Majesty* (Dallas: Word, 1987), and by the writings of Judson Cornwall, *Elements of Worship* (South Plainfield, N.J.: Bridge, 1985); *Worship As Jesus Taught It* (Tulsa: Victory House Publishers, 1987); and *Meeting God* (Altamonte Springs, Fla.: Creation House, 1986).

2

---------- ✧ ----------

Worship and a Changing
World View

*Worshiping churches, sensitive to a dramatically changing world view,
seek to develop a worship open to the supernatural, aware of mystery,
and committed to participation.*

NOVEMBER 1969 WAS A TURNING POINT in my life, a time that I
will always remember and which I am still seeking to interpret and
understand. I was in my second year of teaching at Wheaton College
and had been asked by the chaplain to speak in chapel.

Fresh out of doctoral studies, I was prepared—or so I thought—
to persuade the students of that era of the intellectual validity of the
Christian faith. But I found, much to my dismay, that the intellectual
answers were hollow and unconvincing. Something more was
needed. I knew this in my spirit, but I did not have sufficient experience or adequate language to chart a new course for myself, much
less for others.

So here I was, destined to speak in chapel, desirous to interpret
the spirit of the sixties and anxious to blaze a path for Christianity
to take in the seventies.

I knew my intellectual answers lacked integrity because I myself could not connect my experience with my belief. That fact convinced me that I should not and could not offer the rational answers
of my academic education to a student body hungering for the reality of God in their lives.

As I prepared my sermon, a sense of God's absence kept running through my mind and was validated by my own experience.
God was absent to me, to my inner person and the affective, emotional side of me. Sure, I could reason God's existence and discuss
theological matters with a degree of intelligence, but I felt nothing.

During this time, the Spirit gifted me with a willingness to experience the silence of God—and it was a deafening silence, a real absence of such intensity that I cried out with the fullness of my being for God to become present in my life. "God," I said, "I don't want more information about you. I want you!"

Little did I know what God was doing at the time. Through the sermon I preached on the silence of God, he was moving me to a new—or perhaps I should say "old"—way of experiencing his presence. God was moving me from a purely intellectual understanding based on propositions and analysis to a realized experience of him in worship. In the early church, before there were denominations and varying systems of thought about God, worship was the key to experiencing God. God was experienced as present and active in the worship of the church. God's presence in the worshiping community drew the issues and struggles of life into Christ's death and restored the worshiper to the newness of life in his resurrection.

It was years before I grasped the significance of what had happened to me. Even more years passed before I realized how my experience—and that of others who sense the absence of God in their lives—is closely tied to a vast cultural and spiritual shift taking place in the world today.

I want to describe that shift in culture and show how the silence of God in our lives is related to what is happening in our culture today. My primary concern is not to discuss the shifts in culture, interesting as that may be. Instead, I want to show how culture has affected our worship and created barriers that prevent God from entering into our worship and startling us with the presence of Christ and the power of the Spirit.

Our Secular World

Historians, sociologists, and scientists tell us that World War II marks a turning point in Western history, a turning point so dramatic and far-reaching that we can describe our time now and in the twenty-first century as a new era.

Most people agree that we now live in what C. S. Lewis called "the post-Christian era." What is challenging about our present world is its striking similarity to the time when the Christian faith emerged and took root in the Roman world. Like the days of the early church, ours is a secular and hedonistic age. People are turning to the gods of astrology, occultism, and Satanism. Starved for the supernatural, for mystery and belonging, people rush to the gods of the New Age movement and embrace evil powers in order to experience spirituality.

I believe we Christians must seize the moment and meet this challenge head on. But we cannot confront this age with a truncated and reductionist faith and worship. I don't believe we can engage our contemporaries with a message that is either primarily intellectual or emotional. I am convinced, however, that we can meet the demands of our day with an active faith, a faith that restores the biblical and historical tradition in a contemporary style, that is inviting and participatory, and that brings meaning and healing to life.

This kind of worship is not ancillary to the work of the church, not something done in addition to other ministries. Rather, it stands at the center of the church's life and mission. It is the summit toward which the entire life of the church moves and the source from which all of its ministries flow. It is the most important action the church is to be about. Worship informs the church's teaching, gives shape to its evangelistic mission to the world, and compels the church toward social action. Worship is the context in which the true fellowship of Christ's body is realized and where those who participate can find real healing.

In brief, the single most important thing the church can do is worship. A vibrant worship life will break through the sense that God is absent and reach the people in the world who are searching for meaning. But before we look at this life changing worship, we need to look at worship in the collapsing world of the Enlightenment. We need to understand why so many people find the current worship of some churches spiritually dead and unsatisfying and why God seems to be absent in their—and our—daily lives.

A Static World View and Worship

The world view of Sir Isaac Newton has dominated the Western world since the seventeenth century. In brief, this Enlightenment philosophy offers an anti-supernatural and rationalistic perspective on life. Unfortunately, many Christian groups have developed a faith and worship which accommodates this world view. This old Newtonian view of life relegates God to the heavens and rejects an active presence of God in worship.

Thomas Kuhn, in his influential book *The Structures of Scientific Revolutions,* provides a number of helpful insights that can help us grasp what is happening. With the demise of a Newtonian outlook that sees the world as standing still, we are witnessing the end of a faith and worship characterized by passive noninvolvement, intellectualized propositions, and a seeming absence of God. First, though, a closer look at where we've been.

The Enlightenment World View

We must first acknowledge that the Western world has been living out the Enlightenment story for the last several centuries. And that story goes like this: The world came into existence by chance; it is a huge machine capable of being understood through rational inquiry and investigation; human beings must create the world's future; and the meaning of life must emerge out of the choices we humans make. Perhaps the most important words of the Enlightenment are "reason," "evidence," and "science," words that describe the essential naturalism (as opposed to the supernatural) that has dominated modern Western thought.

The voices of the Enlightenment proclaimed that this world could be understood by the human mind. In time, Darwin introduced the notion of evolution, an idea soon applied to the chance origin of the world and of the human species. Human beings, it was asserted, were not created in the image of God, but evolved from lower species. A new doctrine of creation was born.

Then Freud argued that religion was the invention of the human imagination, born out of the weakness of humans who needed a supernatural crutch to survive life. Now that "man has come of age," society can put away the silly notion of a God, stand on its own two feet, face life with courage and self-assurance, and create its own meaning. A new doctrine of salvation was born.

Finally, Karl Marx, the third influential figure of the nineteenth century, said human beings must take history into their own hands. They must shape their own future by eliminating the competition between the rich and the poor and creating a new communal society where all people will live in harmony under a loving government. A new doctrine of the future was born.

These three seminal thinkers of the nineteenth century played an important role in the development of a world in which God was either dismissed or regarded as irrelevant.

Liberal Worship

Christianity responded to these voices of the Enlightenment by using the tools of the Enlightenment, the tools of reason, evidence, and science. Liberals accepted the anti-supernatural world view and rushed to demythologize the Christian story, rid it of its supernaturalism, and remold it according to the demands of rational thinking and scientific evidence.

Furthermore, in a bold attempt to rescue a supernatural Christianity from embarrassment, the liberals claimed that the story of the Bible was really only a myth which tells human beings how to live. Jesus was no longer "conceived by the power of the Holy Spirit and born of the Virgin Mary." It was no longer true that a complete atonement was made when "he suffered under Pontius Pilate, was crucified, died, and was buried" for our sins. It was no longer believed that the powers of evil had been overthrown in the work of Christ or that "he descended to the dead [and] on the third day he rose again." No! Such antiquated notions belonged to a by-gone supernatural view of life no longer acceptable to the mature thinker of the scientific era.

For the liberals, Jesus Christ was no longer the fulfillment of the messianic hope. No longer was Jesus the one in whom God was present in the world and reconciling the world to himself. And no longer was Jesus accepted as the Messiah who would return at the end of history to judge the powers of evil and free the creation and its creatures from their bondage to decay. Instead, the Jesus of the Enlightenment was a gentleman and an attractive model of what it means to be human. He was the fellow who came to tell humanity about God, to teach people how to live, and to call men and women into a life-style of love and compassion for one another.

But what about the miracles and all those supernatural stories in Scripture? They were dismissed as inventions of the imagination; legends, stories, and myths all told with good intentions. It wasn't that Jesus actually walked on the water or healed the sick or raised the dead. Goodness no! Reasonable people know that this is a closed universe and that the supernatural doesn't operate in it. The "miracle stories" of the Bible simply meant to say, "This man was so great that his followers could only express their feelings about him by imagining that he could walk on water, heal people, and raise the dead."

Liberal worship reflected this anti-supernatural script. Hymns, Scriptures, prayers, sermons, and Communion became acts to inspire people and to enable the human spirit to be like Jesus. And what happened? Because the Christian message and its worship had been emptied of meaning, people left the church in droves. Even today, many churches in the liberal tradition are still trying to figure out what happened. Many of these same churches are waking up to the discovery that where there is no Gospel, there is no Christian worship because there is nothing to celebrate.

Conservative Worship

Unfortunately, the conservative reaction to the Enlightenment story wasn't fully biblical either. It took two forms. One group decided they could prove the Christian faith to be true and set out to do so. The other forsook the mind and opted for emotionalism.

Intellectual Worship

Conservative intellectuals adopted the Enlightenment method of science, reason, and evidence as they set out to prove their faith. "This is a supernatural world," they said, "but because God does not intervene in the world today, we do not look for anything supernatural to happen in worship." They continued, "We think the main task of the church is to defend the Christian faith. Through the use of science, reason, and empirical evidence, the church can prove this to be a supernatural world. Of course this supernaturalism is not evident today. It was only in the first century that God accomplished supernatural acts. He did so then to confirm that Jesus was his Son so people would believe."

For these conservative intellectuals, the task of the Christian faith was to prove the faith and explain it. Consequently, conservative seminaries became intellectual bastions for the Christian faith. Unfortunately, the pastors trained in these intellectual centers wrongly assumed that the pulpit was the place to proclaim the evidence of the faith, dispute with unbelievers, and affirm the faith as verifiable.

Many pastors turned worship into teaching. This worship teaching followed the intellectual style of the Enlightenment: the validity of the Christian faith was presented through logical analysis, Scriptural support, and even scientific evidence, especially from the study of archaeology. Some of these expounders of the truth were gifted not only with good clear minds, but with great oratorical skills and natural charisma. The churches they pastored were full, and even today some churches have success with this approach. It attracts people who like to be intellectually stimulated, but it is not worship in the biblical sense.

I remember going to one of these large teaching-oriented churches on Easter, the day for a great and glorious celebration of the resurrection of Jesus Christ. We the congregation sang "Up from the Grave He Arose," and the choir pleased us with a few rousing Resurrection numbers and "alleluias!" And then came the sermon. The topic? "Thirteen Proofs for the Resurrection of Jesus Christ." I went away empty. I didn't know why. As a matter of fact, I was beginning to wonder if I was losing my faith—I just couldn't connect with those proofs. They meant nothing to my life except that after I died, I would be raised. The proof for my own resurrection is found in the resurrection of Christ.

Nice as that thought is, it didn't do anything for me. It didn't elicit praise, it didn't empower me, and it didn't bring any healing into my life. I simply felt numb, unresponsive, and unmoved by facts about the Resurrection. There was no sense in which I had died with Christ to the powers of evil or that I had been resurrected to a newness which could be experienced in worship, fill my life with meaning, and compel me to live by the fruits of the Holy Spirit. I didn't experience the joy of the Resurrection or any sense of celebration in the people. Worship was dry, dull, and lifeless. *"There's got to be more to it than this,"* I thought. But there was no one there to take me by the hand and lead me to a new place. Everyone at that worship service seemed caught in the same quagmire, the old duty-bound requirement to be at worship—even on Easter Sunday!

Unfortunately, this same pattern of worship, a worship formed out of an evidential Christianity shaped by the Enlightenment, still exists in many of our churches today. Like me, many people are awakening to the fact that "something is wrong." But many don't know what is wrong. And even if they did, they don't have adequate tools to fix it. All they have is a hammer and a crowbar when in fact they need a bulldozer and a crane.

Emotional Worship

The other conservative response to the Enlightenment's mechanistic and closed world view came from the Revivalists. For them, the mind was the greatest enemy of the Christian church and its worship. Christianity, they said, is not something to debate and argue. It is a faith to be experienced. They wanted to be emotionally involved in worshiping their God, not intellectually removed.

A long line of Christians who experienced this kind of involvement populate the modern Enlightenment: the Pietists, the Revivalists, the Holiness Movement, the Black church, the Pentecostals, and the charismatics. For the most part, these worshipers have ignored the Enlightenment world view and the intellectual questions it poses for modern Christians. They aren't interested in getting involved with logical debates, with "evidence that demands a verdict," or with the development of a science that opposes evolution. Instead, they want a Christianity that touches the heart, moves the will, and results in holy living. They want commitment and passion. They want to feel the presence of Christ and experience the power of the Holy Spirit.

Some of the most heart-wrenching, soul-moving, hand-clapping, and body-swinging music of the church comes from these good folks. This tradition has produced the great hymns of Zinzendorf, Watts, and Wesley. From this tradition came camp meetings, soul music, black music, the gospel song, witness songs, and now the praise chorus. This tradition has always valued music as a major vehicle for an immediate sense of the Spirit, and this tradition has always sought to provide people with an experience of God, not merely a reason to believe that he exists.

I have experienced worship in this tradition since my childhood. In my earliest years, my parents were missionaries in Africa, and when they returned to the States, my father became a Baptist minister. In Africa, we sang joyous songs—sometimes to the beat of drums, the rhythm of simple musical boxes, and the movement of dance. I can still remember the gospel song in rural America where uninhibited but poorly trained pianists banged out the tunes on old, scratched pianos characterized by a high, tinny sound. The congregation which bellowed the words was out of tune with the songwriter's intention but in tune with the Spirit. The worshipers, with their eyes closed and bodies swinging slightly to the music, would be lost in wonder and praise. (Back in those days, hand-raising had not yet been introduced.)

The sermons were usually hellfire and brimstone. The preacher paced back and forth on the platform, banged on the pulpit, waved a Bible above his head, pointed his finger, stomped his foot, and did more than a little screaming. And all of this effectively moved the congregation to the highlight of the meeting and the real reason we were there—the invitation. The preacher called all sinners to repent, come to Jesus, receive new life, and become a child of the King.

But like worship that appeals only to the mind, worship that is geared toward an emotional response alone also wears thin. After a certain period of time—it's longer for some than for others—people tire of the antics and long for something more substantial. They want worship that engages the whole person and not just one's emotions. When worship is modeled upon the rich biblical and historical tradition of the church, only then can it offer believers fulfillment they didn't find in a more emotional approach.

Each of these Protestant traditions does, in fact, touch on a necessary element of worship: the intellectual tradition wants truth; the emotional tradition wants personal experience; and the liberal tradition wants impact and relevance to the day-to-day. True worship—worship in which God touches us with his transforming power—must concern itself with all of these dimensions of the faith: truth, experience, and lifestyle.

Of the three responses to the Enlightenment—liberal, intellectual, and emotional worship—the latter tradition, which engages the affective side of the person, is healthier than a be-a-nice-person worship or a merely intellectual worship. Worship which engages our emotions is also closer to the experience of God's presence, to the involvement in worship which biblical worship demands, and to the demands of a more dynamic view of life. And that is the kind of worship now necessitated by the shift into a more dynamic world view.

The New Dynamic World View and Worship

In *A Brief History of Time,* Stephen Hawkins has captured the imagination of his readers by describing the shift from the old Newtonian mechanistic and rationalistic world to a new world view that recognizes the complexity and dynamic nature of all things. In this best-selling book, he exposes us to the New World understanding that results from Einstein's theory of relativity and quantum physics.

In brief, our view of the universe has been revolutionized. The old idea of an unchanged and static universe has been replaced by the notion of a dynamic and expanding universe, a universe that had to have a beginning, will have an ending, and more than likely has a creator. Ideas—particularly challenging ideas having to do with the origin, meaning, and destiny of the universe—have consequences. New ideas in science—in this case, Einstein's concept of a dynamic world—have trickled down into every facet of life and are now in the process of changing our attitudes, behavior, and understanding of ourselves.

The main aspect of this new world view which we must consider—and consider thoughtfully for our worship—is the conviction that the universe is open and not static. Consequently, people are now considerably more open to the supernatural and are searching for an experience of mystery. They are convinced of the interrelatedness of all things and are more relational themselves. They demand participation, are more community-oriented and more process-oriented, and are given to learning and communicating through the visual.

This new world view and the various responses to it certainly pose new threats to the Christian church. One such threat is the rise of the New Age Movement with the religious experiences it claims in its doctrine of reincarnation and its practices of channeling and meditation. These practices have reached into every sector of life— home, school, courts, business, politics, and health, to name a few.

Nevertheless, the challenge to the church is greater than the threat. The challenge is to express and practice a biblical Christianity and worship in the face of current New Age thought. We cannot meet the challenge with a Christianity shaped by the Enlightenment. Neither a liberal mythological faith, a conservative intellectualized faith, or an emotional faith lacking in content will adequately address New Age issues.

Besides being out of step with the contemporary culture, these responses are inconsistent with biblical Christianity. A faith grounded in the Bible proclaims an open universe in which the supernatural does occur and things are interrelated through God's act of Creation. The Bible also acknowledges the importance and ability of human beings to consciously and deliberately participate in life through choice, and it teaches that people need to be in a right relationship with God and each other. Scripture instructs people to be part of the new community, the church, and teaches the necessity of becoming Christlike. The Bible also affirms the role of the visual in communicating truth. In brief, the Bible views the world as open and dynamic. What is needed today is a rediscovery of that world view—not merely understanding it, but experiencing it. And the place where we may experience it best is the corporate body of Christ assembled for worship. It is here that God becomes present to us in our needs.

I find that the worshiping churches experiencing growth are the churches aware of the shift toward a dynamic world view, a shift which they seek to encounter with a worship shaped by the biblical and historical tradition. Unfortunately, many pastors and churches remain untouched by the changing world view and unexposed to biblical and historical sources of spiritual guidance. In light of this fact, we must ask whether or not change in worship is even possible.

Is Change Possible?

I am well aware that many people resist change, particularly in the area of worship. And certainly change in worship will not come easily. I see that as I travel around to do workshops on worship. Two attitudes seem to surface in nearly every situation.

First, I find the strongest desire for change among the lay-people. Occasionally I find a pastor who is ready to take the risk of worship renewal. But by and large, it is the parishioner who longs to break from the old and mechanical, from the sterile and the dead, to experience new life in worship. It is not unusual for a parishioner to take me aside and ask, "What can we do?" or say, "I tried to get my pastor to come to the worship workshop, but he said he is too busy. He really doesn't want to change, but many of us are ready and willing to work toward a more active and biblical worship."

People are ready for such a change because their lives have changed considerably. Their day-to-day world has been influenced by the new world view that has trickled down into every aspect of human experience. People who find the mystery of the universe in their lives, enjoy relationships with friends, participate actively at work or in various organizations, and are accustomed to visual communication in television, advertisements, and supermarkets feel alienated in worship settings. There they bump up against a mechanistic order, a rationalized explanation for everything, a passive, one-way communication, and a service that does not engage their senses.

The second attitude I find during my workshops and travels is caution on the part of many pastors. They are somewhat threatened by the prospect of change. At one of my workshops, for instance, a pastor stood up and said, "I find what you have said to be rather interesting, but I have to tell you I like the way I do it and I don't want to change."

I think there are several very substantial reasons why pastors are hesitant about change. One is that seminary education does not equip a pastor for leading worship. Many seminaries do not even require worship courses or training. The training that pastors do get is in the art of preaching. In fact, almost every course in seminary is oriented around the preaching act. Students learn languages, the Scripture, theology, and church history so that as pastors they may effectively and intelligently present the Word of God. I'm certainly not against good preaching. Indeed, we need more good preaching, not less. But the work of the church is worship in which preaching has its place, not preaching introduced by a few so-called preliminaries. Unfortunately, because of this training and perhaps even because of their gifts, most pastors feel that preaching is the essence of worship. A few outstanding and gifted preachers build the church around their preaching and feel they are quite successful at it, but this is neither biblical nor is it, in the end, a means to good worship.

Furthermore, I feel that most pastors, perhaps because they are somewhat conservative by nature, have a fear of the unknown. I can understand this. There is a security in doing services the same old way, and there is a certain insecurity that comes with venturing into something new and different, particularly when you are leading a variety of people with their own agendas.

In addition, most pastors feel there is a lack of training and resources to guide them into an understanding of worship. What is worship renewal? What does it look like? Where can I obtain resources for worship? How would I use those resources? What steps do I take first? These are very complicated questions that a leader of a congregation must consider. Yet, where there is a real commitment to worship renewal, those questions can be answered, and help in renewing worship can be found.

Finally, unless pastors and people are able to get together and effect worship renewal through prayer and hard work, I fear people who want a renewed worship will simply leave their local church and find it elsewhere. I have already witnessed a growing restlessness among a number of people. More than a decade ago it began as a trickle of people leaving here and there. While I have not witnessed a mass exodus of people from unrenewed churches, there are certainly enough signs of strain and unrest to suggest that this trickle of people may grow into an ever-increasing flow. Such a flow may take a disastrous toll on a church that remains resistant to change in worship.

Conclusion

This chapter has been about the great shift taking place in our Western world today—a shift from the Newtonian world of mechanism and rationalism to a new concept of the world that recognizes dynamic movement and mystery at the very core of life. My point is that worship is undergoing a similar shift. With the old world view, worship was static. It fit the mechanistic and rationalistic mind-set of the world. But now, with people's life experiences changing to include dynamic movement and more participation, a worship that does not also move in this direction will become increasingly tedious and out of step with the world people are living in.

While I am proposing that we change our worship because the world view of our culture is changing, there is an even more fundamental reason for change. Our worship should change because biblical worship is given to participation and mystery. But that will be addressed in the next chapter.

Allow me to close with an incident that illustrates my point. I happened to run into one of my colleagues as I was working on this chapter. When he saw me, he said, "Bob, I've been looking for you. Last Sunday I took my Sunday school class of teenage kids to St. Michael's Catholic Church. [St. Michael's is a renewed Catholic church characterized by a strong participatory worship.] None of us, including myself, had ever gone to a Catholic worship service, and we all expected it to be stuffy, ritualistic, full of 'Hail Marys' and strange things. It wasn't. It was a marvelous service. I sensed mystery. I was involved as a real participant. The music was joyful, and the sermon was short, to the point, and challenging. The Eucharist was a great celebration, and the people even clapped for us when we were introduced."

"What did the kids think of it?" I asked.

"They loved it. To a person, they felt the same things I did—and they want to go back. They couldn't believe how much they could be involved and how joyous the worship was!"

This is not a book about Protestants becoming Catholic or vice versa. And it is not a book about becoming liturgical or leaving your church in search of one that is experiencing worship renewal. That may happen, but it is not something I particularly encourage unless it is obvious that your home church will not change and that being there is detrimental to your spirituality. No. This is a book about worship renewal. And the renewed worship I intend to describe is biblical. It's participatory worship that engages the whole person and is joyous and full of life. Renewed worship isn't in conflict with the new dynamic world view that is permeating our life and all our activities. Renewed worship is worship in which God breaks into our daily lives with his transforming power.

This worship is not owned by a liturgical church, by a praise and worship tradition church, or by any one particular church. It is a worship for the whole church, a worship that has taken root in Catholic and Orthodox churches, in mainline Protestant churches and evangelical churches, in fundamentalist churches and charismatic churches. Nor is it a worship renewal that calls for absolute uniformity. Rather, this renewal thrives in any worship style and finds expression in the particular history and tradition of all denominations and traditions. But most importantly, it is a worship that allows God to break through the walls we have built that keep him out of our worship. This kind of worship allows God to enter our lives and give us direction and healing.

What I propose is not beyond the realm of possibility in your church. I have traveled to, spoken in, and worshiped among people of nearly every major denomination, and I have witnessed the dramatic changes taking place in churches everywhere. This book not only reports those changes but sets forth an easy-to-follow blueprint for worship renewal in the local church. Worship renewal takes prayer, commitment, courage, and hard work, but it's worth the time and energy. Worship renewal results in the renewal of the whole church and in spiritual and numerical growth. Most important, renewed worship brings glory to God.

Bibliography

To understand a world in transition, I suggest reading Thomas S. Kuhn, *The Structure of Scientific Revolutions* (Chicago: University of Chicago Press, 1970) and Stephen W. Hawkins, *A Brief History of Time: From the Big Bang to Black Holes* (New York: Bantam Books, 1988). Kuhn explains the concept of paradigms, how they come into existence, and what they mean. He then introduces the reader to the new paradigm of science and thought today, the idea of an expanding universe.

I am not aware of any books that specifically link the new paradigm of an expanding world with a discussion of the practice of worship. It is sufficient to say that worship renewal in all branches of the Christian faith already reflects the shift into a world of mystery. One sees in churches of all types the return of a more supernatural view of worship and the need for the deliberate participation of all worshipers. These two principles are fundamental to most of the recent books on worship, books that are referred to in other chapters.

3

---◇---

Back to the Biblical and Historical Tradition of Worship

Worshiping churches are drawing from the biblical and historical tradition of worship, especially from the early church's focus on the work of Christ; the recognition that Word and Table proclaim and celebrate the overthrow of evil; and the process of entering, hearing, celebrating, and going forth.

I CONDUCT WORKSHOPS on worship in which many evangelical and mainline churches participate. For the most part, I deal with churches characterized by a passive worship. Worship for many of these churches is primarily a sermon with a few Scriptures, prayers, and songs interspersed. The involvement of the people is limited to the hearing of the Word.

In these workshops I do a modernized version of a second-century service. It is faithful to the general outline of biblical and historical principles of worship, but with a decidedly contemporary flavor. I do this service because I want those attending the workshop to experience a participatory worship with its roots in the origins of Christian worship.

If possible, we meet in a fellowship hall where we can make creative use of space. I want a room that allows for the movement and involvement of all the people. Picture a large hall with a round table at one end and chairs facing each other at the other end. A pulpit is at the left of the center aisle and a place for the worship leaders on the right.

As the Entrance begins, the people gather around the Table singing songs which celebrate this coming into the presence of the Lord. The songs are accompanied by as many instruments as I can elicit from the workshop attendees. This joyful music is designed to be sung from the heart, lifting the worshiper into the presence of God.

We then sing an Entrance hymn as we make our way to the seats on the other side of the room. I ask the people to process together with a hand on the shoulder of the person in front of them and with the rhythm of the music reflected in the movement of their bodies. There is always a lot of joy in this processional, a kind of praise in movement that young and old alike experience. Still standing, we then worship God through a Greeting, Call to Worship, Invocation, Confession of Sin, Act of Praise, and Opening Prayer.

We then sit for the Service of the Word. An Old Testament reading is followed by the singing of a psalm and the reading of the Gospel. I "storytell" the Gospel reading: a first-person account enables the people to participate in the action of the story, to see it, hear it, and feel it in a new way. Then I sit down and ask, "What did you hear, see, or feel in this story?" The people then stand to comment on what they experienced in the story, together creating their own sermon. I'm always amazed by the depth of their insights and the power of the feeling expressed in these short comments. After the sermon, we move to the Bidding Prayers: I bid people to pray for certain concerns, and we pray for them one by one. We listen and pray silently when others pray, and then, at the end of each prayer, together we say, "Lord, hear our prayer."

We then sing another joyful song as we process to the Table where we celebrate the death and resurrection of Christ. Once we have gathered at the Table, but before we begin the Prayer of Thanksgiving, we pass the Peace of Christ. This ancient custom is an expression of God's love to us and of his welcome to the Table, a welcome he extends because of the work of Christ. People greet each other in the name of the Lord, warmly shaking hands or embracing each other.

After the Passing of the Peace, the Prayer of Thanksgiving is said over the bread and wine. The people respond with uplifted hands (a biblical and early church tradition), acclamation, and song *(Sanctus)*. After the prayers, the people walk to the Table to receive the bread and wine. The server calls each person by name, saying, "Sharon, the body of Christ, broken for you," places the bread in the hand, touches the palm of the hand, and perhaps even presses the hand. During this action, all the people join in the Communion Song, singing joyful praise music which expresses the meaning of the Resurrection. In the meantime, those who wish can receive an anointing of oil in the name of the Father, the Son, and the Holy Spirit. The blessing follows: "May the Holy Spirit come into your life and bring healing to you—mind, body, and soul—and may you be filled with the presence of Jesus Christ." The service ends with a benediction, a hymn, and words of dismissal.

This service by no means exhausts the biblical and historical tradition, but its description does allow me to point to several crucial principles for worship renewal, principles which are being recovered by today's worshiping churches. They are: (1) biblical worship is event-oriented; (2) the event of Christ is proclaimed in word and responded to in the thanksgiving offered at the Table; and (3) the process of worship includes four acts: entering into God's presence, hearing God speak, celebrating at the Table, and being sent forth to serve. I believe these principles will help us learn to experience God's transforming power when we worship.

Biblical Worship Is Event-Oriented

I grew up in a home where the Old Testament was honored and Jews were lovingly regarded. For this reason, I remember Jewish friends clear back into my childhood. But I recall the different relationship I sensed the first time I attended a synagogue service. There, in the midst of a Hebrew congregation, I found that I had entered the historical Hebrew tradition that reached clear back to the days before Christ. I sensed I was not only participating in an event, but in an actual history, in a culture brought into existence by God and preserved for centuries in spite of setbacks, losses, and holocaust.

I discovered through my experience in the synagogue that the worship of Israel is rooted in the Exodus-event. I experienced how, through the retelling and the drama of the Exodus-event, Israel continually actualizes its own existence as the people of God. In that worship, my Jewish friends became once again the people of the Exodus-event.

I'm convinced that the most important feature of Hebrew worship is that it is rooted in an event. If you were to ask a Jewish person, "What is the most significant event in your history? What event defines you and gives shape to your existence in the world?," the answer would be the Exodus-event. Here is where God acted for

Israel, bringing Israel up out of its bondage to Pharaoh. Here is where God entered into relationship with Israel and constituted Israel as a special and unique people bound to God on the basis of a covenantal relationship.

Hebrew worship recalls the Exodus–event and looks forward to the Promised Land. As this true story is rehearsed again and again in various ways, God is praised for his faithfulness. Remembering the faithfulness of God, the people are to live out this story, allowing its hope to shape their personal and corporate lives.

What Is Christian Worship?

Like Hebrew worship, primitive Christian worship was very event–oriented. This connection to Hebrew worship is only now being rediscovered by current biblical and liturgical scholars. So there remains a great deal of confusion about the most fundamental question worshiping churches must address: What is Christian worship?

I recently spoke to Tim Mayfield, former director of worship for the General Baptist Convention. Pastor Mayfield had just returned from a conference on worship where he had challenged the ministers to focus their energy on worship renewal. I asked, "In your mind, what was the most important point you made with these pastors about worship renewal?" He answered quickly and without hesitation: "I told them, 'Get your definition of worship straight. Everything you do in worship renewal will flow out of that definition.'"

I fully agree with Pastor Mayfield's advice. The practice of our worship today is directly related to what we believe worship to be. If a church claims worship is teaching, its worship will consist of a few "preliminaries" and a long sermon. If a church sees worship as evangelism, its entire service will move toward the invitation. If a church views worship as essentially praising God, it will worship primarily in song, relying especially on those songs that praise God for his transcendence and holiness. Is worship teaching? Is worship evangelism? Is worship singing? Or is worship all of this and more?

I have struggled to define worship in a way that is faithful to the biblical and historical event-orientation, and I have discovered that worship is not easy to define. Worship is a multifaceted action that can be described in many ways. Even the above descriptions are not completely wrong. Biblical worship does teach, it does evangelize, it does extol God. The problem with basing worship on just one of these definitions is that it limits worship. When worship is defined in terms of a single aspect, the worshiping community is locked into developing a worship style that focuses on that one truth. And that's what we see. One church emphasizes preaching, another evangelism, and another praise. What we need is a definition of worship that, rather than limiting worship, is broad enough to include all aspects of worship.

What has helped me most is to recognize truncated definitions of worship frequently come out of the question, "What should worship accomplish?"—and that is the wrong question. As soon as that question is posed, worship planners think in terms of goals: worship should teach; worship should evangelize; worship should heal; worship should entertain; worship should lift up God. Then, to accomplish the stated goal, planners order and organize worship around the goal. This goal-driven approach to worship is, I believe, ineffective because it does not operate out of the biblical vision of worship.

Since my own background and prejudice have always been toward a goal-driven worship, I struggled for years to develop a comprehensive definition of worship. One day as I was meditating on the worship of Revelation 4 and 5, the definition which I had run across a dozen or more times in scholarly literature finally became clear to me. What I saw in the vision of St. John was a worship focused on Christ and his work of redemption. I realized in a new way how God is praised and glorified as the work of his Son is told and enacted again and again. As I reflected on that Scripture, I saw that the biblical question is never "What does worship accomplish?," but "What does worship represent?"

The heavenly picture of worship is clear: Worship represents Jesus Christ through re-presentation. Worship tells and acts out the living, dying, and rising of Christ. Worship celebrates Christ's victory over evil, the certain doom of Satan, and the promise of a new heaven and a new earth. A brief yet comprehensive definition of worship is worship celebrates God's saving deed in Jesus Christ. This kind of worship is not a goal-driven worship, but a Christ-driven worship. And when Christ is the center of worship, all of the goals for worship are achieved: Christ-centered worship educates, evangelizes, heals, develops spirituality—and is most enjoyable.

A Christ-centered worship—which is event-oriented worship—can never be static and merely intellectual because what happens is an actual and real communication of the power and benefit of the life, death, and resurrection of Christ. Worshiping churches recognize that every gathering of worship is ultimately a praise and thanksgiving for the overthrow of evil by God in Christ. This victory not only happened two thousand years ago, but it happens today in the lives of people who bring to worship their own struggles against that evil which shatters relationships, oppresses the poor, and brings constant dislocation into life.

The event of Christ is the only event in human history that promises relocation and centering, meaning and purpose. The promise and its fulfillment evoke passionate and heartfelt praise and thanks, especially for those aware of their own brokenness and the healing which Christ brings into their lives. For this reason, worshiping churches are returning to the biblical focus of worship—a celebration of the work of Christ characterized by a spiritual immediacy that touches people where they are. In this kind of worship, God breaks in and becomes present to touch our lives and create us anew.

Biblical Worship Centers on Word and Table

The earliest stories of Christian worship tell of worship in the synagogue and worship in homes. Synagogue worship focused on the Word while home worship was ordered around the breaking of the bread. In these two institutions of worship, we find the origins of both our Service of the Word and our Service of the Table. Allow me to take you back to the first century so that you can experience worship as it may have happened among early Christians. Imagine for a moment that you are a first-century Christian living in A.D. 40, ten years after the Resurrection. What is it that you see, feel, and experience in both synagogue worship and home worship?

When you enter the synagogue, you greet your friends and neighbors and then sit down to prepare yourself to hear the Word of the Lord, the Old Testament Scriptures. The synagogue contains all the symbols of your rich history, and you gaze on them in preparation for worship. You remember that the building itself, which faces East, is a symbol of God's promises to Israel and of the coming of the Messiah—a promise fulfilled, you believe, in the person of Jesus. Your eyes then move to the front of the building and settle on the Ark that houses the written records of God's activity in your history. You note the veil protecting the scrolls in the Ark and the seven-branched candlestick with its flickering flame. These symbols remind you of the presence of God in your own Hebrew history as well as here in this place.

Your eyes now turn to the bema, the raised reading platform in the middle of the synagogue around which chairs are placed. Here the Scriptures will be read, the prayers said, and the Scriptures explained. Again, you recall how the Scripture and its proclamation symbolize the presence of God. Now you know that this God of the Word who becomes present through the reading of the Scripture actually became present in Jesus of Nazareth, the man crucified and proclaimed by many to be the Messiah.

Now you look at the seat of Moses. Soon a rabbi will sit there. He will expound the Scripture and enter into debate about this Jesus of Nazareth. You know that the rabbi who will speak today does not believe Jesus is the Messiah. For him, the symbols of the synagogue and the Scripture have not yet been fulfilled: the Messiah is still to come. He does not see in the symbols the same things you see. He sees the Old; you see the New. And in the discussion of Scripture after the rabbi's explanation, other Christians will challenge his interpretation for in it they, too, see the New and not the Old.

Soon synagogue worship is over. As usual the worshipers have debated over the Christ, and some hard feelings have resulted. Family, friends, and neighbors are divided over the issue. So you look forward to the celebration of the New Covenant in the house where the Christians now meet.

You enter the house, greeting your friends with enthusiasm. It is good to be among those who won't be debating about Jesus. You know that together you will experience his presence in worship.

The house meeting begins with an agape meal, a love feast in which the Jewish prayers of Shabbat are prayed. These prayers, which you have heard in your home all your life, will be changed slightly to express the conviction that Jesus Christ is the Messiah. As you gather with others in the home, your eyes fall on the rich variety of tasty food set on the Table around the bread and wine.

Before you eat, the host—in the tradition of the Jewish Shabbat—raises a cup filled with wine. He prays, "We give you thanks, our Father, for the holy vine of David, your servant, which you have made known to us through Jesus, your servant." You and the others respond, saying, "To you be glory forevermore." The wine is passed around, and you drink some. A similar prayer is said over the bread, and it, too, is passed around and eaten. You then get in the food line along with everyone else, talking, laughing, and enjoying the company of other believers.

After the meal, the leader may lead the congregation in psalm singing. An Old Testament passage or two may be read and discussed. Or perhaps an apostle may be visiting, and he'll tell stories about Jesus, interpreting his death and urging you to live a life pleasing to the Lord.

Then come the prayers, after which the leader will say, "Maranatha!" which means "Our Lord, come." These words signal the beginning of a brand new rite, a thanksgiving offered to God the Father for the Son and for the new life that comes through his death and resurrection. You will say new prayers connected with the bread and wine. These elements were once symbols of food for the body, but now they are symbols of food for the soul as well. By participating in this offering of bread and wine, you know that you are participating in Christ's death and resurrection. Christ died to destroy the power of evil, and you participate in his death by allowing the power of his death to come into your life and put to death the evil that you struggle with. Just as Christ's resurrection was a resurrection to a new life, you surrender to the power of the Resurrection in your own life. You allow God to release the Spirit of joy, peace, long-suffering, kindness, goodness, faithfulness, gentleness, and self-control within you. This is not only the Thanksgiving of the church, but yours too. It is your Eucharist, your offering of thanks to God the Father.

In this imaginary early Christian worship experience—which scholars believe is a fairly accurate picture—we see the biblical precedent for both the Service of the Word and the Service of the Table. There is a sense in which the Word read and preached in Christian worship always celebrates the New in the Old. And there is a sense today in our worship at the Table that we are always celebrating the fulfillment of the Old in this new rite.

For this reason, worshiping churches are maintaining the centrality of the Word in worship and are adding to the Service of the Word the great response of thanksgiving at the Table, a response to the Word which goes back to the very beginning of Christian worship. Here the church praises and gives thanks to God for the work of Christ who dethroned evil at the cross and who now in worship gifts the worshiper with victory over sin by the power of the Spirit.

The Four Acts of Worship

As time progressed, the early Christians recognized the need for Acts of Entrance and Acts of Dismissal in worship. Consequently, historical worship is divided into four movements: (1) We enter into God's presence; (2) We hear God speak; (3) We celebrate at God's Table; and (4) We are dismissed.

The Four Acts of Worship

Word		*Table*	
We enter into God's presence	*We hear God speak*	*We respond with Thanksgiving*	*We are dismissed to love and serve*

These four movements of historical worship have been recovered in worship renewal today. A brief description of each will help us grasp the contours of a biblical and historical worship.

1. We Enter into God's Presence

A number of years ago when I first became conscious of the convergence of worship traditions, I organized a workshop for leaders from liturgical, traditional Protestant, creative, and charismatic traditions. The grand finale of the entire conference was a service in which each of the traditions was responsible for a distinct part of worship. For this service, I felt that the praise tradition charismatics could provide the best leadership for the Entrance. Because an Entrance should be full of joy, I naturally gravitated to the praise tradition people whose contemporary songs and choruses are exuberant and enthusiastic.

I told the worship leaders: "Bring us into the presence of God with great joy. Help us experience what Israel experienced when they came into the Temple with all the musicians, trumpeters, and singers giving praise and thanks to the Lord. Make us ready to hear the Word of the Lord with a grand and glorious entrance."

I emphasized how the Entrance "makes us ready to hear the Word of the Lord." For this reason, it should last long enough to accomplish its task but be short enough that we are not exhausted when we arrive at the hearing of the Word. Unfortunately, my praise tradition friends did not listen to me and conducted a fifty-minute Entrance, leaving us all enervated by the time we came to hear the Word.

The point is that an Entrance should bring us joyfully into the presence of God and ready us to hear him speak. It should not overshadow the Word because we are in worship not only to praise God, but to hear the story and have it applied to our lives.

2. We Hear God Speak

The Service of the Word, the second movement of worship, begins when we are in the presence of God. Here, the story of God's action in the world is told through Scripture readings and the sermon, and we respond to it with various acts of worship.

Sometime ago, when I was doing a workshop in Massachusetts, a Methodist minister told me how he "storytells" the gospel every Sunday and how his people love to hear the Scripture in a fresh new way. Many pastors whom I've told about this method confirm how alive the gospel becomes for people through the art of storytelling.

What I look for in the Service of the Word—and what is happening more and more in renewing churches—is a lively presentation of the Word. I want someone to read who knows how to read, and I want the person who preaches to communicate to me. Whether the Scripture reading and the preaching are done formally as in a liturgical or traditional Protestant church or informally as in a creative or praise and worship tradition church is not of ultimate importance. What is crucial is that we hear the Word of the Lord. If Scripture is proclaimed in a rote manner and if the sermon is preached either as if it is a painful exercise we have to endure or is presented in pious platitudes for comfortable religious people, then the meaning of the Word is lost and worship is not happening. Scripture and sermon are historical recitations of how the God who acted in history acts now in our lives. People need to experience the immediacy of the Word of God. They need to know that the God who acted in history can be active now, touching their lives, healing their hurts, and giving them a vision for the future.

3. We Respond with Thanksgiving

Not long ago I was in Irvine Presbyterian Church, pastored at the time by Ben Patterson. This church, like many renewing churches, has increased the practice of the Table, knowing that it is both biblical and practical. Christ is especially active at the Table to bring healing into the lives of those who are open to God's work in worship.

Because Pastor Patterson understands the service at the Table to be the church's great response of praise and celebration to the Word, Irvine Presbyterian Church has broken with the mistaken funeral dirge approach to the Table. Instead, the ancient motif of celebrating the Resurrection has been restored through hymns and choruses. I love to sing—and hear singing—during Communion because it joins me with all who come to receive the bread and wine. Singing together is a mysterious form of communication that helps us to truly experience the presence of God and his transforming power that means healing and restoration through Christ.

At Irvine Presbyterian Church, worship leaders also provide an opportunity for the laying on of hands and prayers of healing. I noticed how many people, after receiving the bread and wine, stopped to receive prayer as they returned to their seats. I asked Pastor Patterson about offering prayers for healing in connection with the Table of the Lord. "How have the people responded to this practice?" I'll never forget his answer. "Bob, it is one of the single most important aspects of the ministry here. A lot of broken lives are touched. People look forward to that special opportunity for prayer, and God is healing the lives of many through that sacred action." When we come to God in a state of vulnerable openness, God breaks through and touches our lives. This happens especially at the Table of the Lord.

4. We Are Dismissed to Love and Serve

The final act of worship is the Dismissal. The people have entered joyfully into the presence of the Lord; they have heard God speak; they have responded to God by giving thanks over bread and wine; and they have been touched by the renewing presence of God. Now they are ready to be sent out into the world where the action of loving and serving God is a continuation of their worship. Here is the place where I like the announcements. There is a sense in which our gathered worship is over. Announcements about what this body is going to do during the week are appropriately a part of worship and, I think, most appropriately a part of the sending forth.

The Benediction follows. In renewal worship today, the Benediction has been revived as a vital part of worship. It is understood, as it was originally, to have real spiritual effects. The Benediction is proclaimed as a work God will do in the lives of the worshipers as they allow worship to mold and shape their lives during the week.

Chuck Smith, Jr., the pastor of Calvary Chapel in Capistrano Beach, California, spends a great deal of time thinking and praying through the Benediction. A few years ago, I worshiped in his church, and I still vividly remember the benediction and how powerfully it blessed my going forth. Pastor Smith has put some of these benedictions to writing. Here is one for the first Sunday of Advent:

> Now may the mighty God,
>   Ruler of heaven and earth,
>   Watch over your life
>   And give you protection this new week
> May his Spirit fill you with the hope
>   of knowing that his Son,
>   our Lord Jesus Christ,
>   is soon to appear.
> And may that hope
>   help you to become a better person
>   who knows God,
>   performs his will,
>   and gives him praise
>   both now and always.
>
> Amen.

After the Benediction, worship continues with a hymn that sends the people forth into the world. The choice of hymns is important.

At one of my workshops, a woman came to me and said, "My pastor has us sing praise songs after the Benediction. Somehow I don't feel this is an appropriate place for songs of praise and adoration. What do you think?"

I think she is right. Each movement of worship serves a different purpose. The purpose of the Dismissal is to send us forth. Praise songs belong elsewhere. This is a time to sense the charge of God in our lives, and the dismissal hymn should do that.

Many renewing churches are concluding worship with what is called Words of Dismissal. This tradition, borrowed from the liturgical service, adds a powerful touch to the meaning of the Dismissal. The words often used are "Go forth into the world to love and serve the Lord." And the people respond with a hearty, "Thanks be to God."

Conclusion

Worshiping churches are not only sensitive to a dramatically changing world view, but they also seek to develop a worship faithful to the biblical and historical tradition.

In this chapter, I have pointed toward that biblical and historical tradition of worship and commented on three aspects crucial to worship renewal. First, worshiping churches in every denomination are rediscovering the event-orientation of worship. Leaders recognize that biblical worship celebrates the death and resurrection of Christ and that this celebration must connect with our lives so that, by identifying our sins, struggles, and failures, we might identify with Jesus and experience our own resurrection to a newness in life. Second, in worshiping churches, this saving, restoring, and renewing event of Christ is proclaimed through both the Word and the Table, the two historic institutions of Christian worship. Third, churches aware of their historical roots celebrate the life-changing Christ-event in four movements: worshipers enter God's presence, hear God speak, celebrate God's work of restoration at the Table, and are sent forth into the world to love and serve the Lord.

These three points by no means exhaust the biblical and historical tradition. More about early Christian worship and its ability to meet the needs of worshipers will be presented in future chapters. But, before looking at this worship in greater detail, let it be said that many churches are finding that God uses this ancient approach to worship, revitalized for today, to break into people's lives with his transforming power.

Bibliography

For the sense of mystery and the holiness of God in worship, see Rudolf Otto, *The Idea of the Holy* (New York: Oxford, 1977). This book contains an excellent discussion of the debate between Eunomius and St. John Chrysostom as well as long excerpts from Chrysostom's work *De Incomprehensibli*. The biblical teaching concerning Christ as the focus of worship is explained well in H. Grady Hardin, Joseph D. Quillian, and James F. White, *The Celebration of the Gospel* (Nashville: Abingdon, 1964). Unfortunately, the book is out of print and is available only in seminary libraries.

I also suggest Michael A. Cowen (ed.), *Alternative Futures for Worship: Volume 6, Leadership Ministry in Community* (Collegeville: The Liturgical Press, 1987); David N. Power, *Gifts That Differ: Lay Ministries Established and Unestablished* (New York: Pueblo, 1985); and a book of the Twenty-Third Conference Saint Serge, *Roles in the Liturgical Assembly* (New York: Pueblo, 1981). These three books discuss preconditions for worship renewal—specifically, community, participation, and mutual ministry—from a Catholic point of view. Since many of these same questions are addressed by Protestant communities, the material in these books is valuable for Protestants as well.

For a broad understanding of Jewish worship, see A. Z. Idelsohn, *Jewish Liturgy and Its Development* (New York: Schocken Books, 1960). More specific matters of Jewish worship are addressed in J. H. Kurtz, *Sacrificial Worship of the Old Testament* (Grand Rapids: Baker Book House, 1980); Joseph Stallings, *Rediscovering Passover: A Complete Guide for Christians* (San Jose: Resource Publications, 1988); and Geoffrey Wizoder, *The Story of the Synagogue: A Diaspora Museum Book* (New York: Harper & Row, 1986).

For an understanding of the relationship between the Old and New Testaments, see C. W. Dugmore, *The Influence of the Synagogue upon the Divine Office* (Westminster: The Faith Press, 1964) and Martha Zimmerman, *Celebrate the Feasts: Of the Old Testament in Your Own Home Church* (Minneapolis: Bethany House Publishers, 1981).

Good insights into New Testament worship are presented in Oscar Cullmann, *Early Christian Worship* (Chicago: Regency, 1953) and in Ralph Martin, *Worship in the Early Church* (Grand Rapids: Eerdmans, 1974). An excellent study on Table worship is found in Joachim Jeremias, *The Eucharistic Words of Jesus* (Philadelphia: Fortress Press, 1966).

For early church studies, I suggest Josef A. Jungman, *The Early Liturgy: To the Time of Gregory the Great* (Notre Dame: The University of Notre Dame Press, 1959); Gregory Dix, *The Shape of Liturgy* (London: SacrePress, 1945); and Willy Rordorf, *The Eucharist of the Early Christians* (New York: Pueblo, 1978).

4

---◇---

The Contemporary
Convergence of
Worship Styles

Worshiping churches freely borrow from other worship traditions. As a result, the four main traditions of worship today—liturgical, traditional Protestant, creative, and praise and worship—are undergoing a convergence of style.

IMAGINE VISITING a stately liturgical church, a church with vaulted ceilings, marble floors, beautifully appointed oak, stained-glass windows, a carved altar and pulpit decorated with figures of the saints, the clergy dressed in brightly colored vestments, and the smoke of incense rising toward the heavens. In the midst of this splendor and beauty, people begin to process to the altar. As you join them and move toward the front of the church to receive the body and blood, all of you lift your hands and sing, "We love you, Lord, and we lift our hearts to worship you."

Impossible! you say.

Now imagine entering a traditional Protestant church with gleaming white walls and stark wooden pews stained in oak. The pews are trimmed in bright white to match the pulpit, the Communion table, and the trim of the choir loft. Large chandeliers hang from the ceiling, and a bright red carpet runs across the highly polished wood floor up the center aisle and the steps of the raised platform where the furniture of worship—the Communion table, pulpit, and baptismal font—is highly visible. The minister, banner bearer, and choir are assembled in the back, all dressed in white robes. The Entrance hymn begins, and the procession is led by a dancer who, through the motion of his body, expresses the joy of coming into the presence of God.

Unheard of! you say.

Next, imagine joining a worship service in a typical evangelical church. The pews have been taken out so the people can be seated in a circular fashion around the large Communion table and highly visible pulpit. The service begins with praise music accompanied by a band and lead guitarist. When it is time for a sermon, you expect a forty-five minute exegetical explanation of a Scripture passage. Instead, the pastor "storytells" the gospel. You are riveted to your seat as you hear, see, feel, and experience the story in a new way. It's not just a story of someone else, but a story that makes vital connections with your own life. Then the pastor sits down and says, "What did you hear God saying to you in this story?" All of a sudden you feel your heart pounding a little bit harder because the Scripture clearly spoke to you and you know you should share what you heard with others. You stand. . . .

Never! you say.

Now imagine being present in a praise and worship tradition/ charismatic church. The church is plain and simple with theater seats arranged in the half round. A band is to the right and a piano and synthesizer to the left. Mikes and other electronic equipment are visible but discreet so as not to be intrusive. After beginning with typical praise and worship songs, the worship leader says, "The Lord be with you" to which all the people heartily respond, "And also with you." Then, at the end of the prayer, all say loudly, "Amen!"

Doubtful! you say.

Finally, imagine that in each of these settings you felt the presence of Christ. Your heart was truly warmed by the love of the community, and you were fully engaged in the action of worship. You sang, you prayed, you heard the Word, you celebrated at the Table, and your spirit was lifted. You knew that you ministered to God from your inner being as God ministered to you, bringing you peace and delivering you from fear, anxiety, and the temptation to be calloused, jealous, envious, materialistic, and selfish.

The various scenarios described above are happening across America and around the world. I call this phenomenon "the convergence of worship traditions." The body of Christ is coming together in a renewed worship that freely borrows from the various traditions of worship.

This phenomenon is breaking down the walls of denominationalism. Consequently, renewing churches of every denomination may now be classified into four broad worship traditions: (1) liturgical worship, (2) traditional Protestant worship, (3) creative worship, and (4) praise and worship tradition worship. Allow me to illustrate what is happening in each of these traditions.

1. Liturgical Worship

I recently received my first invitation to speak on worship in an Eastern Orthodox church. Although I've worshiped in Orthodox churches before, I wasn't quite ready for what happened there. While the people were receiving the bread and wine, the entire congregation began singing together the choruses I usually associate with the praise and worship tradition. Hands were lifted up and people were lost in the praise and wonder of God. They were fully and consciously participating in the mystery of God's healing presence made available at the Table.

Often, when people characterize liturgical worship, they think of a fixed order, written prayers, classical music, a short sermon or homily, a weekly Eucharist, and the church year. Liturgical worship is criticized for its ritualism, dead orthodoxy, and vain repetition; for being merely a rote recitation of the words of the prayer book. The charge of ritualism may be fair for some churches, but not in renewing churches. Worshipers there see the prayer book as an order which organizes heartfelt worship to God, an order that is not closed but instead contains open spaces where they may respond to what God is doing in worship. For such a church, the charge of ritualism is simply not true.

My first experience of liturgical dance in an Episcopal setting is another example that counters the charge of ritualism. At the offertory when the bread and wine were brought to the Table, a dancer led the procession. Through the movements of her body, she made alive the drama of setting God's Table in preparation for the church's feast of the Resurrection. This was no performance, no mere praise in motion designed to entertain us. Rather it was movement that served the text. The text was the symbolic coming before the Lord with ordinary bread and wine that would be returned to us as symbols of the body and blood of Christ, given in death and Resurrection so that we might have life. I found myself joining in that dance: I participated by sight. And I experienced an inner spiritual peace as I gave myself again to God through that offertory dance.

I have also found that the prayers of the people—called the bidding prayers in the liturgical church—are quite participatory. I did a workshop for a group of Protestants from Boston in a monastery in Hingham, Massachusetts. Joining the monks in their worship, we were able to experience firsthand the joy of their renewed worship. I remember especially the involvement of all the people in the prayers of intercession. The priest said, "I bid you to pray for the sick and those in need of the guidance of the Holy Spirit." I expected the silence which happens in some churches or, at best, a few prayers spoken aloud but softly. I was, however, quickly drawn into the prayer life of that congregation as, one by one, many people prayed passionately for those who were ill or in need of the Spirit's direction. These were prayers from the heart, each of which ended with the words, "Lord, in your mercy," to which the entire congregation responded, "Hear our prayer." I thought to myself, "These people have been taught to pray!"

Then there is the passing of the peace. In many liturgical churches, this experience has become an opportunity to express the real love and fellowship experienced in the community. Recently, in a small Episcopal church of about one hundred people, I was overwhelmed by the passing of the peace, an experience that became a great Christian hug-in. People left their seats and, for five minutes or more, passed the peace of Christ. They shook hands warmly and embraced joyfully. This was no mere secular greeting, but a real experience of God's love and of God's welcome in the body of Christ.

I have also experienced a marvelous moving of God's Spirit in the great Eucharistic prayer. I was in an Orthodox church once when everyone in the church closed their eyes and lifted their hands in worship at the cherubic song, a song sung at the beginning of the Eucharistic prayer. In my home church, St. Mark's Episcopal, something very powerful happens when we sing the *Sanctus*. I feel a shift in the intensity of the Spirit. And as I walk forward to receive the bread and wine, sometimes to the singing of "Just As I Am" or a moving Taize Scripture chorus, I always feel that I am once again saying "yes" to Christ's work of redemption for me.

Also, it is not uncommon in liturgical renewal to offer the anointing of oil with the laying on of hands at the Communion table. I've been in churches where, immediately after the reception of bread and wine, a deacon or person with the gift of healing offers the laying on of hands with prayer for healing. In other churches, prayers for healing are conducted at the altar rail after the service is over.

What is happening in these liturgical churches is very simple and basic. People are discovering that liturgy was never meant to be a closed order with no room for spontaneity. Instead of being a closed and fixed order, liturgy is really a guide. Taking the worshiper by the hand, the liturgy leads the worshiper through a joyous Entrance, a meditative hearing of God's Word, a celebratory experience of the Table, and a sending forth into the world. This more open liturgy renews the worshipers' Christian experience as they consciously and deliberately participate in worship. This participation makes the celebration of God's saving deed in Jesus Christ real, personal, and joyous.

2. Traditional Protestant Worship

The Overland Park Church of the Nazarene is an elegant brick, wood, and glass sanctuary that sits proudly on Lamar Street in the spacious city of Overland Park just outside Kansas City, Missouri. Under the leadership of Pastor Randall Davey with the insightful assistance of Dr. Paul Bassett, professor of history at the nearby Nazarene seminary, this church has experienced a virtual turnabout in worship over the last several years.

As I entered this house of worship through the large glass doors that beckoned me, I was greeted by a husband-and-wife team who made certain I felt welcome. I followed the people in front of me up the steps toward the sanctuary where once again I was greeted warmly and made to feel at home.

Since I like to sit in the front, I made my way to the second pew, took my seat, and bowed to pray in the silence that prevailed. After my prayer, I noticed that the large cross in front was set against a rugged stone wall behind the pulpit. The choir area was draped with a large purple cloth, sending forth the message that it was Lent. On cue, the ministers in the front row stood to their feet and walked to their places of leadership to begin the worship.

The Acts of Entrance began as the minister said the simple statement, "On this the fifth Sunday of Lent, let us worship the Lord." I wondered how many Nazarene churches observe Lent, but I soon lost the question as I joined with others in singing the psalm of the day selected from the lectionary. As soon as the psalm ended, the organ provided leadership for the *Gloria Patri*. The congregation sang with great gusto—they truly wanted to give glory to God. Next came the processional hymn "I Sing the Mighty Power of God." Led by the organ and three fine trumpeters, the congregation sang lustily as a gala procession of more than forty robed choir members made their way to their seats. For me, this was a moving experience of coming into the presence of God, and I sensed it was for the entire congregation as they came before the Lord with committed intentionality.

Pastor Davey then led us in a prayer of confession, asking God to forgive our sins, to assist us in mending our ways, and to lead us into a holy way of living. In another prayer, the forgiveness of our sin was accepted in recognition that God cleanses those who call upon the name of the Lord. Then came an act of praise by the choir, the singing of the hymn "I Will Praise You." We responded to their praise by confessing that Christ is risen and singing "All Hail King Jesus."

As I was singing, "I'll sing your praises and I'll reign with you throughout eternity," I thought of how the Acts of Entrance had ordered my experience of coming before the Lord and how I was made ready to hear the Word. These acts of worship, drawn from liturgical and praise and worship tradition sources, had been skillfully woven together with elements of the Nazarene tradition and were enthusiastically entered into by all the people.

Next came the Service of the Word. The lectionary readings carried us through an Old Testament reading, a hymn of response, an Epistle reading, and another hymn of response, bringing us to the cherished Nazarene tradition, prayer at the mourner's bench. In this particular church, this is the time for the prayers of the people, a time for people to identify the dislocations in life with which they are wrestling and a time to relocate in the love and tender care of God. Pastor Davey quietly moved to one of the two prayer benches located at the front of the church and knelt. Without receiving any word of invitation or explanation, a dozen or so people quickly made their way to the benches and knelt. A man in front of me, weeping softly, walked to the bench and hunched over it in a posture of grief. While most of the people remained in their seats, all bowed and some slid to their knees.

The pastor's prayer was followed by the Lord's Prayer, a prayer that has become quite meaningful to the members of this church. As one member told me, "We have been taught to be accountable to God and to each other. We have made an intentional choice to be under the authority of the Lord's Prayer. I travel a lot in my business and I need to live especially by the words 'and lead us not into temptation.' I have a brother to whom I'm accountable for my actions, and, when I return from my trip, he wants to know if I was led into temptation."

The pastor used passionate and eloquent language in a prayer that brought all of us into the very presence of God. We were able to take to God our lives, our families, our work, our hopes, and our failures, and we knew that he had heard us and touched us with his love.

Later at lunch I said to Pastor Davey, "I'm trying to figure out how each worship tradition allows for God to touch the heart of the worshiper. I sense that the mourner's bench is key in your worship. Is that true?"

"Yes, it is," Pastor Davey said. "As a matter of fact, the mourner's bench is often used after worship as well. It's a place where a person wrestling with a problem is able to receive the anointing of oil and special prayer for the breaking in of God on their lives."

The morning service ended with a "comma," for that evening the people would return to celebrate at the Table of the Lord and be dismissed to serve the Lord with gladness during the week. I left my visit at Overland Park Church of the Nazarene with the sense that this traditional Protestant church had effectively integrated historical and contemporary resources for worship with the particular traditions of the Nazarene church in a way that provided a fulfilling and meaningful worship experience for its rapidly growing membership.

Overland Park Church of the Nazarene, a traditional Protestant church, represents those worshiping communities whose worship is not quite as fixed as that of the liturgical church and not quite as free as those with a more extemporaneous style. On the right are those churches influenced by Calvinism (the Reformed churches and the various branches of Presbyterianism, for instance). On the left are those churches that can trace their roots to John Wesley, as do the Nazarenes, the Christian Missionary Alliance, and the Methodists. It is somewhat difficult to say which church fits where since many influences have affected particular denominations and local churches. Consequently, Reformed, Presbyterian, and Methodist churches cannot all be classified in one particular way. A Reformed church, for example, may be quite free and informal in its worship while a Methodist church might be quite liturgical. On a spectrum from liturgical to free church, these nonliturgical denominations and their specific local communities fit somewhere in between. Some lean more toward liturgical worship while others lean more toward free worship.

What specifically is happening in these denominational groups and the churches related to them?

First, the traditional Protestant denominations of the mainline church have produced some very significant resource materials such as supplemental liturgical books. I am particularly impressed with the common structure of worship that has emerged in these materials, a structure that goes back to the early church and seeks to bring about a reform of worship based on the spirit and practice of worship in the early centuries. These materials recognize worship as a reenactment of the great salvation acts of God. And, like Overland Park Church of the Nazarene, the materials follow the ancient order of worship where believers joyfully enter into the presence of God, hear and respond to the Word of God, celebrate at the Table of the Lord, and are sent forth to serve. The specific infrastructure of these four parts of worship may change from one denominational resource to the other, but each group seems to be paying careful attention to these sequential acts of worship and to the differing mood that each act expresses. It is clear that these churches are borrowing from the liturgical tradition. When introduced into worship, however, these ancient resources do not take on the character or style of a so-called liturgical worship.

Traditional Protestant churches are also enjoying a revival of the arts. I was recently involved in a community ecumenical worship service, a service celebrated in a Methodist church to welcome the arrival of Advent. The Entrance hymn was "O Come, O Come, Immanuel." A dancer led a procession carrying a number of tastefully appointed Advent banners. The art—the dance and the banners—effectively served the sense of Advent: I saw designs and movements which expressed waiting in eager anticipation. I don't remember the sermon, but the Entrance Acts made a deep impression upon me. Now, much later, the procession remains vivid in my imagination because it set into motion my Advent spirituality and a genuine longing for the coming of Christ.

Besides adapting worship elements from the early church and rediscovering the value of the arts, many traditional Protestant churches are turning toward a more complete and frequent celebration of the Eucharist or Holy Communion, as it is still called in many of these traditions. Recently I worshiped in a Presbyterian church where it was obvious that the Table of the Lord was not merely tacked on to the end of the service. In this church, as in many other Reformed churches, Communion is no longer a quarterly practice. Instead it is celebrated monthly with worship leaders hoping to eventually celebrate the Table weekly. Furthermore, the text of the prayers used in Communion has been closely worked out according to the ancient canon of Hippolytus, A.D. 215. In this Presbyterian church, the prayers were dialogic; the congregation sang as the bread and wine were served; and two elders, a man and a woman, stood in front of the sanctuary on either side to offer prayers for healing.

This Presbyterian Communion service was very moving. I sensed a spirit of celebration and expectancy in the songs and in the movement of the people as they processed to the Table to receive the bread and wine. Many of the worshipers stopped to receive the laying on of hands and prayer, and they seemed profoundly moved by the experience. After the service, I asked the pastor if such responses to worship were typical. He answered, "Yes. You have no idea how pained the lives of many of my people are or how much healing of broken hearts and lives goes on there at the Table through the ministry of healing. It is my conviction—and my experience confirms it—that God breaks through especially at the Table to bring healing and salvation into our lives."

This church and many other traditionally Protestant congregations are clearly drawing on the classical resources of Christian worship. They are also discovering the contemporary arts and including songs from the praise tradition. Finally, the services I am aware of, like that of Overland Park Church of the Nazarene, are characterized by a good balance between order and freedom, and these services actively draw worshipers into full, conscious, and deliberate participation, engaging the whole person in worship.

3. The Creative/Contemporary Model of Worship

Willow Creek Community Church, the second largest church in the United States, is about a thirty-minute drive from my home, so I occasionally attend its Wednesday and Thursday evening worship time. (Sunday morning is used for outreach.)

Driving to the church is itself an experience because several thousand cars converge on the parking lot in a relatively short period of time. The last time I went, I felt as though the bumper-to-bumper traffic served as a kind of procession leading into worship. Allowing that journey into the parking lot to be a procession, I felt my worship with the people of this church had already begun before I found my place among them in the sanctuary.

After the prelude, worship leader Joe Horness stood up and said, "Good evening and welcome to Willow Creek. Hebrews 13:15 says, 'Through Christ, then let us offer up a sacrifice of praise to God. That is, let us offer him fruit of our lips, giving thanks to his name.' Tonight we have another great opportunity to offer God our sacrifice of praise, so let's stand together and begin by doing just that!" We stood and sang choruses that lifted our sacrifice of praise to God in joyful sound and enthusiastic praise.

After greetings and announcements, an elder's report, the Scripture reading, and a drama, Joe stood to his feet again and addressed the community. "The phone rang last night. It was a close friend of mine calling to tell me that his company is moving to California. Either he moves, or he is out of a job. . . . I played racquetball with another friend of mine whose young son is handicapped. He shared with me how life for him these days means just making it through one day at a time.

"Psychologist Scott Peck opens his book *The Road Less Traveled* with the profound observation that 'life is difficult.' And every one of us tonight could share some story about an area of our lives where those words ring far too true—life is difficult! All of us, to one degree or another, need a sense of God's comforting touch somewhere in our lives."

After saying this, Pastor Horness asked us all to look at Psalm 3 printed out in the bulletin and to identify anxieties in the spiritual, personal, relational, vocational, and material areas of our lives. For a full five minutes, we silently meditated on this psalm and on the crises we were facing in our own lives. When I looked around to see whether or not people were serious about identifying their own problems and struggles, I saw some people bowed in prayer, others writing, and many more in a state of transfixed meditation. The sanctuary was quiet, ever so quiet, as God was allowed to work in that space provided for the creative activity of the Spirit.

Pastor Horness then asked us all to stand and sing of God's providing, healing power. We sang, "Come unto me all who are weak, weary, and heavy laden; gentle am I, humble of heart, and you shall find rest for your soul." I could sense people coming to Jesus with their anxieties and concerns, laying them before the Lord. Then we sang several more songs—"He Is Our Peace," "I Cast All My Cares upon You," "You Are My Strength," and "Not By Might."

After the service, I spoke to Pastor Horness, "Are you aware of what was going on tonight?"

"What do you mean?"

"You helped these people identify their dislocations, and then you relocated their lives in God," I said.

"That's true," Pastor Horness responded. "After worship, one person came to me and said, 'My wife is leaving me and I don't know what to do,' and another person said, 'I just heard my business is going bankrupt.' And both of these people told me, 'I'm so glad for the worship tonight because I've gained perspective on my life and a new trust in God.'"

Creative worship, like that of Willow Creek Community Church, seeks to meet the felt needs of people in worship, to lift them out of their dislocations, and to relocate them in God and in the hope one can have in the midst of life when they trust in him. In worship like this, churches are helping people hear the voice of God in their lives and open themselves to a touch of transcendence.

More and more, Willow Creek Community Church and churches like it seem to be moving toward including the worship styles of other traditions. In March 1990, for example, Pastor Bill Hybels of Willow Creek presented to his congregation a Roman Catholic priest as a "brother in Christ" and interviewed the priest for the Sunday morning message on the subject "What Protestants Can Learn from Catholics." When the priest spoke about the importance of the Eucharist for his own spirituality, Pastor Hybels strongly affirmed the need for Protestants to restore a sense of the presence of Christ in worship, especially at the Table of the Lord. Pastor Hybels pointed out how Christ breaks through the seeming silence of God in our lives with the healing and comfort he offers us in our worship at the Table.

4. Praise and Worship Tradition/Charismatic Worship

Several years ago I gave a series of talks on worship to the faculty of a praise and worship tradition college. My lectures had to do with the need to rediscover the rich treasury of resources from history, to include all forms of music in worship, to increase the celebration of the Table, to recognize the evangelical nature of the church year, and to incorporate the arts in worship. These points were enthusiastically received, and many persons told me that praise tradition worship was moving to incorporate more and more of the historical aspects of worship into the local church.

The distinct contribution of praise and worship tradition/charismatic worship is its openness to the Spirit. Although some groups as well as some local churches have taken the matter of the Spirit to extremes, the general desire to experience the moving of the Spirit in worship is making an impact on worship renewal in general. This openness to the Spirit is seen, for example, in the recovery of physical freedom (lifting hands, dancing in the Spirit); in the efforts to restore the ministry of believers in worship (the laying on of hands for prayer); and in the restoration of healing in the context of worship. All these aspects of worship have their roots in the early church, and vestiges of these actions have remained in liturgical books of worship appearing here and there throughout history. Today, these elements of worship are common to many renewing communities, evidence of the Pentecostal/charismatic movement's enormous influence on worship. It is, however, a matter of great interest to me to realize how many charismatic pastors feel the need for more structure, more content, and more connection with the past. I find a growing interest among charismatics in the contributions other traditions may make to worship.

Pastor Doug Mills from Gatlinburg, Tennessee, found himself questioning his own people's rejection of the rich tradition of worship. He felt this to be "one of the greatest weaknesses of the charismatic church." In a personal letter to me, he wrote, "I began to feel the pressures of performance-oriented ministry. I felt I had to come up with something new, heavy, deep, funny, or profound every week." He continued, "I came to a clearer realization that the Spirit has been with the church throughout history. I began to see that some of the traditions of the church must have been inspired by the Spirit and therefore pleasing to the Father. It seemed like an obvious truth. I just had never thought through it."

Pastor Mills then began to make changes in the church: "One of the first things I did was to include the Lord's Supper on a regular basis. . . . From quarterly, we went to monthly; from monthly, to the first and third Sundays. . . . At the last elders' meeting, it was decided that we were going to weekly Communion." In addition, the service now includes a psalm and more Scripture reading, and the church has begun to follow the Christian calendar.

I asked, "What has been the impact of this worship?"

"Our worship has become fuller and deeper. . . . We are realizing the significance of being a part of God's universal church. . . . We are becoming a less selfish people. . . . Our people are characterized by a healthy 'fear of the Lord' [and] we have been able to continue to learn and develop in the area of worship without losing the life and vitality of the Holy Spirit."

Richard C. Leonard of Christian Life College, a charismatic school in Illinois, is equally concerned about rediscovering the riches of the church's worship tradition without losing the Holy Spirit. Concerning music, he says, "There is a certain value in the rediscovery of the wealth of Christian hymnody—the majestic hymns of the Reformation, the virile psalm paraphrases of Geneva and the Puritans, the poignant hymns of the American frontier, and the best coinage of English and American hymnists of the nineteenth and twentieth centuries." The point is that praise and worship tradition people are incorporating more and more elements from the historic tradition of worship in their own worship.

Conclusion

While each of the four styles of worship described above reflects a particular tradition of worship, each of them is now influencing the others. The worship experience of many Christians is no longer isolated to a single tradition. Instead, a kind of cross-fertilization is occurring, and each tradition is borrowing from other traditions. I have attended evangelical services which borrow from the liturgical tradition, liturgical churches which are recovering the importance of preaching, and Orthodox services which are borrowing music from the charismatic tradition. I am convinced that borrowing, done intelligently and with spiritual sensitivity and then wisely integrated into worship, can have a powerful positive effect on a congregation's life.

We live in a time when, to the delight of nearly everyone, the Berlin Wall of separation between people has come tumbling down. There is a movement among the people of the world to find out about each other's traditions and to share from each other's experiences. We the people of the church have even more reason to learn what is happening in other worship cultures and to draw from each other's spiritual insights and experiences. After all, there is only one church, and although there are a variety of traditions and experiences within this church, each tradition is indeed part of the whole. The movement toward the convergence of worship traditions and the spiritual stimulation which comes with borrowing from various worship communities are the results of the worship renewal taking place in our time. I am convinced that God is using this borrowing not only to enrich our worship, but more importantly to communicate to us, to break through the silence of our lives, and to let us know that he is there to touch us and make us whole.

Bibliography

Although the convergence of worship traditions is too young to have produced a great number of books presenting and explaining it, several books are available which can help the reader see how renewed worship is drawing from other traditions. Mary Collins, in *Worship Renewal to Practice* (Washington, D.C.: The Pastoral Press, 1987), addresses some of the problems caused by the changes taking place in worship, particularly in the liturgical tradition. Mary Collins and David Power (eds.) in *Liturgy : A Creative Tradition* (New York: Seabury Press, 1983) tackle the issue of change in worship in various periods of history, in various traditions, and in various cultures. Thomas Anderson Langford III in *The Worship Handbook: A Practical Guide to Reform and Renewal* (Nashville: Discipleship Resources, 1984) provides guidelines to help a worship committee put together a worship service using various sources. And Jack W. Hayford in *Worship His Majesty* (Dallas: Word, 1987) shows how the charismatic tradition can successfully draw from the liturgical tradition.

Six Areas of Convergence Worship

5

✧

Preconditions for Worship Renewal

The worshiping church sets aside a time specifically designated for worship; has a clear understanding of the gospel; experiences the church as the body of Christ; develops a community of social relationships; and releases all its members for mutual ministry.

A NUMBER OF YEARS AGO I served as chairperson of the Search Committee whose task it was to find a new pastor for our church. At the first meeting, I suggested we approach the search from the bottom up, not from the top down. Most churches focus their search on finding a pastor who will come in and lead the church: that's a "top down" search. I suggested that we not begin by looking for a pastor, but by examining our church. I suggested that we ask where God was leading us and, once we had a sense of our direction, look for a pastor traveling the same path. That's a "bottom up" approach.

We met regularly for three months with one single question in mind: What is this church called to be? During this time, no mention was made of possible candidates or what kind of pastor we wanted. Our prayers and discussions were only for discernment and direction.

We also committed ourselves to study the New Testament and church history to find the common ministry of the church, a ministry to which all churches are called. Our study brought us to the conviction that the church is called to six ministries. The church, we concluded, is called to be a:

Worshiping Community   *Teaching Community*
Fellowship Community   *Mission Community*
Healing Community   *Servant Community*

We evaluated the strengths and weaknesses of our church in light of these callings and attempted to outline our future direction. We first decided that none of these six God-given ministries was to be ignored and, second, that the church's primary task—the calling from which the other five actions of the church should flow—is the commitment to be a worshiping community. Armed with this conviction, we went in search of a pastor who felt called to provide worship leadership as the primary ministry of the church.

I have shared this sixfold calling of the church with my students and with pastors in various conferences. It always amazes me to discover how few pastors have these six callings in mind as they pray about, think about, or serve the church. Again and again, pastors who are eager to experience the fullness of God's calling in their work ask me to list these areas of ministry and comment on them.

As we talk, I ask pastors to evaluate the strength and weakness of their own ministry in light of these six callings. Invariably, several pastors acknowledge worship to be a weakness, even in the Sunday morning hour. Many pastors admit that their Sunday service is primarily one of teaching or one of evangelism. I'm certainly not opposed to Sunday morning teaching or evangelism. Some churches do this rather well. But I always ask pastors of these churches, "When do you worship?" This question helps pastors discover that there really is a difference between the church teaching, the church evangelizing, and the church worshiping. In the process of recognizing this, many pastors come to the painful realization that they lead a church which does not have a time set aside for worship.

I personally became aware of the lack of worship twenty years ago when I was involved in a church that had turned morning worship into a virtual lecture. Worship was a few songs and a long exegetical sermon. I found this experience so painful that I often went home with knots in my stomach and a feeling of anger about church. I wanted to worship, to praise God, to be touched in my inner person. But, week after week, worship was another lecture. I finally left that church in search of an experience of worship that touched my inner person.

This story raises a very important point which every church must think about, and that is this: A church that would enjoy worship renewal needs to set aside a time for worship.

Setting a Time for Worship

I have been greatly impressed that Willow Creek Community Church, located in the suburbs of Chicago, openly acknowledges that what they do on Sunday morning is not worship. Sunday morning is used for evangelism, for the communication of the gospel through the arts, especially through a creative form of music and drama. At this writing, more than 15,000 people attend Willow Creek's Sunday morning evangelistic thrust called "seeker's service."

Recognizing the need for believer's worship, the church has designated the midweek service (now held on both Wednesday and Thursday nights) as worship. At this time, the committed Christians and members of Willow Creek Community Church gather for believer's worship.

The significance of this decision is that a time has been reserved when the church gathers to worship, and everyone in the church knows that this is the time when they meet for this purpose. Since having a time set aside for worship is imperative, I suggest you gather the leaders of the church and say, "Here are the six ministries of the church. Let's set aside a time for each and make sure that one of those times is labeled 'worship time.'" Most churches find Sunday morning to be the best time for worship, but a church like Willow Creek Community Church may, for one reason or another, designate a time other than Sunday morning.

Once this time has been designated, a local church must attend to four other matters before making any attempts to introduce changes in worship. In this chapter, I will speak about these preconditions for worship renewal.

I have talked with ministers and church leaders who have made slight changes in their order and practice of worship and who, because of these changes, feel they have entered into worship renewal. Some feel they have renewed worship because they now sing choruses, have added the visual arts, or have increased the celebration of the Table of the Lord.

Worship renewal is not primarily changing the order of worship, introducing new elements, or even celebrating the Eucharist more frequently. Worship is the church celebrating the gospel. It is the people of God gathered to become the body of Christ and to experience their own death to sin and resurrection to a new life.

Through that kind of worship experience, God teaches his people how to live out the pattern of dying to evil and being resurrected to Christ, providing continuous renewal for believers.

Appropriating the Gospel

A church seeking to experience God in a renewed worship must first identify its own experience of and attitude toward the gospel. Worship which truly celebrates the saving deeds of God in Jesus Christ is celebrated best by those who have personally appropriated it.

I have always been interested in the story John Wesley told about his own conversion to the gospel. In the famous journal entry, he writes that even as a preacher he did not know the forgiveness of God in his own experience. He had met a group of Moravian Christians who urged him to experience the gospel. At their insistence, Wesley began to seek an experience of faith until finally, on an evening when he attended Aldersgate Church, he experienced a feeling of forgiveness while the Preface to Luther's Commentary on Romans was being read. In that worship, God broke through the silence Wesley had sensed even as a minister and brought him to an experiential grasp of the gospel.

Wesley's experience is not an isolated case. I know of pastors who feel they did not experience the gospel in its personal power until they were already ordained and ministering in the church. Alden Hathaway, the bishop of the Episcopal Diocese of Pennsylvania, tells how he as a liberal pastor decided to preach from the Bible and how, through the study of the Scripture in preparation for preaching, he became personally converted to Jesus Christ. This kind of experience is important not only for the pastor and staff, but for everyone in the church because worship is inextricably linked to the meaning of the work of Christ for the individual.

I tell my students that there are three complementary ways to view the work of Christ in the New Testament, three ways that influence our understanding and practice of the gospel. The first is *Christus Victor* (Christ has dethroned the powers of evil and will utterly destroy them at the end of history); the second is rooted in the notion of sacrifice (Jesus was sacrificed to be an atonement for our sin); and the third is the example model (Jesus, who laid down his life for others, is our example of how to live). These three views of the work of Christ proclaim the Good News which worship celebrates.

The Good News is that the power of the Evil One has been overthrown by Jesus Christ and that we gather in worship to celebrate this overthrow and apply it to our own lives; that a full and complete atonement for our sins has been made and that in worship we receive the continual benefit of this atonement; and that Jesus has left us an example to follow, an example which is proclaimed and urged upon us in worship through Scripture reading and preaching.

A church congregation that desires worship renewal needs to consider these three perspectives on the gospel. A pastor may lead his or her congregation to clarify their understanding of the gospel by asking, "What difference does it make in your life that Christ has defeated the powers of evil? What difference does it make in your life that Christ was sacrificed for your sins? What difference does it make in your life that Jesus left you his example to follow?"

These questions should be dealt with in such a way that a congregation feels and experiences the gospel, not as a one-time experience, but as an ongoing challenge to their experience. Their struggles against the various principalities and powers, their personal defeats, and the dislocations of their life need to be connected to the overcoming power of Christ.

In worship, we bring these dislocations in life to the gospel. We hear and experience how Christ relocates us first by forgiving our sins. Through the Holy Spirit, Christ also enables us to deal with the persistent pressures of evil and empowers us to live in obedience to God's will for our lives.

Good worship involves both what we bring to worship and what worship brings to us. Worship brings the gospel to our needs. In other words, if church leaders are serious about worship, they must have a clear sense of the struggles their people are bringing to worship and of the ways the gospel as it is presented and celebrated in worship addresses these struggles. Worship is essentially the voice of the gospel meeting the voice of humanity in all of its struggles, failures, sins, and painful disorientation.

Experiencing What It Means to Be the Church

In my travels among worshiping communities, I have been greatly impressed by the renewalists' interest in rediscovering the meaning of the church. I'm not certain that every pastor and church involved in worship renewal even understands what's happening, but churches undergoing renewal are rediscovering the church as the people of God.

Recently I was at The Church on the Way in Van Nuys, California, where Jack Hayford is the pastor. Because I was early for the nine o'clock service (there are four services in two different church buildings), I seized the opportunity to talk to some people about their experience in the church. "What is it," I asked, "that you like so much about this church?" The answers invariably pointed to the sense of community—"I feel like I belong," "This is home for me," "I'm part of what's going on here," "This is my family."

What's striking is that these answers focus on the context from which worship derives. While worship celebrates Christ, it takes a community of people to do that work of celebration. The study of the origin of the faith makes it clear that the unique event of the living, dying, and rising of Christ was marked by the coming into being of a body of people, the church, the people of the event. Peter explains it in these words: "You are a chosen people, a royal priesthood, a holy nation, a people belonging to God—" (1 Peter 2:9 NIV).

These words do more than describe the church. They point to its calling to worship. You are a people, a church, a community, writes Peter, "that you may declare the praises of him who called you out of darkness into his wonderful light." The link between the Christ-event, the church, and worship is clear: the work of the church is to celebrate Christ's death and resurrection. That is the very event which brought the church into existence, shapes its people, and defines its meaning and purpose in the world.

But the church that would be about experiencing God in worship renewal must first rediscover what it means to be the church. The church is not an institution, but an organism: the people of God who are the body of Christ. I suggest that a pastor and the leadership of the church study 1 Corinthians 12 to help develop a way for the people to experience this reality. The challenge is to enable the people of the church to truly love each other and to be a genuine community, a body that functions together in life and in worship.

And this challenge is made more difficult by the spirit of individualism characteristic of our Western world. The rugged individual who stands on his own two feet is valued over a group of people working together. This spirit of individualism is particularly strong in North America and derives from the frontier movement as well as the spirit of democracy. As much as we all enjoy our individualism, it is a liability when it comes to experiencing a biblical model of the church.

The church simply is not an aggregate of individuals who happen to come together at a given time to worship in their own individual way. The church is community, a household of faith, brothers and sisters in Christ, the body of Christ. These New Testament images are powerful pictures not only of what the church is in itself, but particularly of what the church is in worship.

Many years ago, when I first became aware of the need to experience God in worship, I left a church that was resistant to worship renewal and became involved in a house church. House churches have the luxury of being small and able to meet in the hospitable environment of a home. In that intimate setting, house churches can concentrate on building a community.

In our house church, worship was always done in the context of a full agape meal followed by an afternoon of playful activity. We grew to know each other well as we shared in each other's problems and joys and as we ministered to each other's needs in some very powerful ways. Because of the intimacy we shared with each other, I was always worshiping among friends who cared deeply for me and for each other. I was not a lonely or completely anonymous individual worshiping in the corner of the church building.

There are those who argue that anonymity in worship is important for some people. I'm aware that a person, burned out from this or that experience in a particular church or from an event in life, may need time to be left alone. Most churches allow for this. But the need for belonging is fundamental. The need to belong goes deeply into the very nature of redemption and touches on matters pertaining to the gospel. There really is no such thing as Lone Ranger Christianity. Christianity is community and belonging, a membership in the new order of things.

A community of brothers and sisters in Christ is better able to experience God's transforming power in worship. Without an understanding of what it means to be the church, believers run the risk of individualistic worship, a worship that is not fully biblical nor completely satisfying to the soul.

Developing Strong Social Relationships

Once a church has begun to understand what it means to be the people of God, the body of Christ, the next step is to develop a community of social relationships. Church leaders need to take an active role in helping cell groups come into being. These groups, which meet together regularly, are characterized by strong social relationships between people who are mutually committed to one another. In a community like this, worship can be renewed.

Not long ago when I was teaching on worship renewal in a local church setting, I mentioned the importance of cell groups. I explained, "This is where people, meeting in small groups, will experience the feeling of family, an experience which will feed into the worship of the larger body. Public worship is a corporate action. If you don't know anyone and you feel as though you are among a group of strangers, your worship will not be as free and expressive as it could be if you feel the warmth, the acceptance, the support of a family group."

I was amazed when someone said, "I've never heard of a cell group. Sounds interesting and important. Could you tell me more?" The idea of cell groups for Bible study, prayer, ministry, social action, and good fellowship is as old as the Christian faith itself and has been frequently used by the Holy Spirit in various revivals throughout history.

The Church on the Way has organized cell groups that meet in more than seventy different homes in the Los Angeles area. Every person attending the church receives a pamphlet urging them to be part of a cell group because "being a regular part of a Life-Net group is as much a part of the body-life at The Church on the Way as attending the weekly services here in the sanctuary. Both the larger services and the affiliated ministry that happens in homes are a part of any growing church vitally committed to the fullest expression of New Testament life." Life-Net is the network of the small groups of the Church on the Way, and its published mission statement says:

> The purpose of Life-Net is for the local community of believers at The Church on the Way to gather in homes under trained leadership to sing, praise, and worship God in the power of the Holy Spirit; and in that power minister to one another in love in such a way that the needs of God's people are met, bring-

ing them to wholeness, enabling them to give in resources and services as we take the city for God.

I spoke to Mark Weinert who is in charge of small groups at Willow Creek Community Church. He said, "I'm convinced that if we did not have small groups, the zeal, intensity, and authenticity of our worship would not exist as it does." Certainly the research I have done among worshiping churches affirms his view and leads me to urge all local pastors and church leaders to organize small groups for ministry and service as a precondition to worship renewal.

Releasing Each Person for Ministry

The next step in preparation for worship renewal is making certain that the gifts and talents of every member of the church are put to good use. This work will begin in the small groups and extend to worship.

Many of the small groups at Willow Creek Community Church emphasize discipleship. A married couple, for example, that has achieved some maturity in the Lord is given the responsibility of discipling three other couples; or a single person disciples a group of singles. According to Mark Weinert, this model for discipleship is based on the relationships Jesus had with his twelve disciples. In such a context, people are able to discern the gifts they can offer the church and the work of Christ.

"Visualize," Mark said, "Christ with his twelve disciples. He didn't just sit around teaching them the Sermon on the Mount— they did it. They lived together, ate together, shared all kinds of low as well as peak experiences. He taught them about forgiveness; then he forgave. This is the model of our small groups. We want our group leaders to model their gifts and talents of discipleship so that someone will take a friend to the steam room at the YMCA and share Christ in the midst of everyday living."

When I was at The Church on the Way, I attended the new members class to find out what they were being taught. (They have two new members classes twelve months of the year with around one hundred people enrolled each month.) The class was titled "Ministry: An Integral Part of Body-Life." One of the points on the handout sheet was "Using the analogy of human anatomy, no single member of our body can function, let alone survive, without the consistent service of those other members with which it is co-joined (1 Cor. 12:12-31)." In this class, each person was urged to give their time and service to the work of the church as more than one hundred different ministries in which they could become involved were presented on paper and discussed.

The concept of ministry is much more biblical than the idea of task, committee, job, or function. Unfortunately, we have organized many of our churches to fit the model of a corporation, and we expect excellence and efficiency from everyone. This secular language suggests that church involvement is merely doing work or performing a duty. We need to return to the biblical concept of ministry, recognizing the different callings people have in the body of Christ and releasing them to minister—not as efficient members of an institutional structure, but as members of a community of love.

The church that cares about experiencing God in worship is a church that will seek to discern its people's gifts and then set them free to do the work of the Lord in the context of God's community, the church. Worship that grows out of such mutual ministry will not belong only to the clergy or be distant from the people. It will be a worship of the people and by the people.

Setting a time for worship, appropriating the gospel, experiencing the church community, developing strong social relationships, and releasing members to their own ministries—these preconditions for worship renewal bring people to the full, conscious, and deliberate participation in worship.

The Participation of All People

Even as the preconditions are being met, one of the most difficult challenges of worship renewal is getting the people involved as true participants. I have been in liturgical, nonliturgical, and even charismatic churches where I could sense the passiveness of the people. They seemed cool and distant not only toward worship, but also toward God. Invariably they were unfriendly and uninterested in me, the visitor. Getting a smile, a handshake, a warm greeting, much less an invitation to dinner was out of the question. But the situation is different in a church where the people are fully, consciously, and deliberately participating in worship.

Several years ago, my two daughters were students at Westmont College in Santa Barbara, California. One weekend when I was visiting, we visited St. Athanasius Orthodox Church, located near the campus of the University of California, Santa Barbara in Isla Vista. I hadn't been there before, but I knew some of the priests and leaders of the church through various contacts.

As we walked into the vestibule of the church, a friendly person greeted us, asked our names, and invited us to sign the guest register. We walked into the service which had already started. People were jammed into nearly every seat, but a friendly usher took us to the front where we sat crammed among several other people, most of whom nodded their heads toward us and smiled as we found our seats. Someone nearby helped us find our place in the prayer book, and we were soon able to join in the singing and the prayers.

The service was a modified version of the ancient St. John Chrysostom service dating back to A.D. 380 and was sung in three parts—the leader, the choir, and the congregation. The tunes were easy to follow. Some of them were ancient plain chant, some familiar hymn tunes, and some gospel songs and choruses. The entire service moved like a drama, and we were caught up as participants in the script, each of us having our parts. Everyone seemed to play his or her part with faith, concentration, and great joy. So strong was their joy that, not far into the service, my oldest daughter leaned over and said, "Dad, they really love each other here!"

Indeed, the unity of the people in worship not only revealed their full and conscious participation, but it gave one a clear sense that these people cared about each other. They threw themselves into this worship for the sake of each other's joy. Somehow, the praises and responses were so clearly communal, passionate, and joyful that my spirit—and I know those of others—were lifted into the glories of the heavens. It was as though we were standing around the very throne of God, joining in a hymn of unending praise.

During the announcements, we were introduced by name along with other visitors (obviously the reason for signing the guest book before the service). After the service, three families invited us to have dinner with them.

I came away from that service with the sense that I had truly worshiped. The good liturgy, stimulating sermon, wonderful music, and warm, hospitable spirit all contributed to my worship experience. Importantly, though, I also felt that I had joined—mind, body, and soul—with others to fully, consciously, and deliberately participate in worshiping our God.

Churches that want to experience God's transforming power in their worship must not overlook the importance of each individual's wholehearted participation. Such participation is necessary to worship renewal. In fact, it can be said that worship which does not demand such personal involvement on behalf of every believer is not worship renewal. Worship is never something done to us or for us, but always by us. Therefore, the church that desires worship renewal must pay careful attention to its worship, giving people permission to participate and providing them adequate ways of truly becoming involved in worship.

Conclusion

If a church has not attended to the matters spoken of in this chapter—setting aside a time for worship; appropriating the significance of the gospel on a personal level; experiencing the church as the body of Christ; establishing cell groups for discipleship, ministry, and fellowship; and discerning and calling forth the gifts of everyone for mutual ministry—I suggest focusing on these matters for at least a full year before attempting any changes in worship. Because worship is done by the people, it must be characterized by their complete and wholehearted participation. This goal is realized only after the members of the congregation have become aware of the gift of community given to them by the Holy Spirit. We do not worship in a vacuum. We worship out of community and in community. Once the importance of the community has been recognized and the congregation has begun to move toward the biblical ideal, then and only then can the people begin to attend to worship renewal. Then and only then can the people be prepared to experience the presence of God in a new and heightened way.

Bibliography

To rediscover the "Christ is victor over the powers of evil" aspect of the gospel, an aspect that is highly pertinent to the contemporary world with its occult and New Age perspective, read Gustav Aulen, *Christus Victor* (New York: Macmillan, 1969) and Hendrik

Berkhof, *Christ and the Powers* (Scottsdale, Penn.: Herald Press, 1977).

To understand the church, one needs to grapple with the New Testament images of the church. I suggest Paul S. Minear, *Images of the Church in the New Testament* (Philadelphia: Westminster Press, 1960). Avery Dulles deals with various historical shapes of the church in *Models of the Church* (New York: Doubleday, 1974), and Paul Henson, *The People Called* (San Francisco: Harper & Row, 1986), shows how the New Testament people of God sought to worship the true God and follow his ways of righteousness and mercy.

An excellent book for small groups is Emory Griffin, *Getting Together: A Guide for Small Groups* (Downers Grove: InterVarsity Press, 1982).

To identify the gifts of the people in your congregation and to free them for ministry, read Frank Tillapaugh, *Unleashing the Church* (Ventura: Regal Books, 1982).

6

◇

Experiencing God's Transforming Power on Sunday Morning

The worshiping church defies the Enlightenment's intellectualized worship and establishes an open worship in which God can act. These churches base worship on the principles that in worship we celebrate Christ, that divine action occurs in worship, and that we respond to God's action by faith with open hearts.

I TEACH A COURSE on worship in the Wheaton Graduate School, a course which draws students from the many traditions of Christianity represented within the student body. The course is organized around six different services from various periods of history: New Testament worship, early Christian worship, Reformation worship, early American worship, praise tradition worship, and a model for future worship. The students are responsible for leading these services, and after each service we reflect on the experience.

In 1990, student Greg Wilde, a charismatic, illustrated how God's transforming power can touch our lives. He conducted a service of binding Satan. This is not a regular part of charismatic worship, but a service done on various occasions.

We met on the second floor of the Billy Graham Center in a space at the center of the building known as the Commons. Graduate students gather here to read their mail, lounge on the sofas, and chat with each other. The sofas had been moved aside, allowing space in the middle for the forty students of the class to congregate for worship.

During the Service of the Word, we were told to claim the victory of Christ over the powers of evil to the north, the south, the east, and the west. We were then instructed to stretch out our arms in those directions when prompted and to pray passionate, evocative prayers claiming Christ's powers against evil.

Only four or five of the students in the class were from charismatic backgrounds, so I wondered what kind of response this highly active form of worship would elicit. As we turned from the east, to the north, then to the south, and finally to the west, I was quite moved by the eloquent and passionate prayers and the power of our actions.

We were doing what worship does: We were proclaiming the victory of Christ over the powers of evil. A divine action was happening as we worshiped. Our prayers were not idle talk or mere discursive speech, but a performatory language, a vivid, colorful description of the victory of Christ over evil and the claiming of people, territories, and institutions for Christ. Furthermore, we were responding to the action, affirming Christ's claim in our own lives and appropriating the victory of Christ in our own personal struggles.

I do not advocate the binding of Satan as a regular part of morning worship, but I do heartily support the principles of worship that this binding represents: worship celebrates Christ; in worship there is a divine action; and we must respond to God in our worship. But before I comment on these three principles, I need to say something about the axiom that experience precedes knowledge. Understanding this axiom will help us discover a new aliveness in our worship as we practice the principles discussed here.

Experience Precedes Knowledge

Many of our churches are operating under the notion that knowledge precedes experience. As a result, they have become almost completely knowledge-oriented and would, I think, be skeptical and fearful of the charismatic service celebrated by my students. Let me explain this more fully.

I was educated in the Enlightenment philosophy, a view which espouses the priority of knowledge to experience. As far back as I can remember, I was told, "Get your thinking straight and your behavior will fall in line." This approach to life—which was everywhere when I was growing up and being educated—spilled over into the church and influenced spirituality, evangelism, and ethical behavior. The church's main job, it was believed, was to teach right doctrine, instill biblical principles, and make certain everyone knew the Christian faith. And then, it was argued, people would live right.

I support the need to have a clear understanding of doctrine and biblical principles, but I question the Enlightenment adage that a person arrives at experience through knowledge. This view has the cart before the horse and has resulted in a highly intellectualized worship which appears closed to any of God's actions other than the enlightenment of the mind.

Before any further discussion of worship, knowledge, and experience, consider the way knowledge is shared. Modern communication theory recognizes two ways, broadly speaking, to communicate. The first is called discursive communication. Discursive communication is informational. You find it in lectures, in books, and in the media. The primary concern is to pass information from one person to another. This is the kind of worship one finds in churches influenced by the Enlightenment.

But there is another kind of communication called communal or cultural communication. This communication has as its concern the formation of the person and community, not just the sharing of information. Communal communication is older than discursive communication. Long before print, formal lectures, and electronic media, there were communities. Early civilization was made up of various tribes, groups, or social alliances. We all know about Abraham and his tribe, the twelve tribes of Israel, and the primitive church. Each of these groups passed down their way of life from one generation to another primarily through shared experiences. The experience of the group, the common heritage of the tribe, the stories and oral traditions of the family—these were the means of forming and shaping lives.

The early church stood in the tradition of communal communication rather than discursive communication. The Fathers expressed it in Latin: *lex orandi; lex credendi; est.* Literally translated, the phrase means "the rule of prayer is the rule of faith." Another way of expressing this idea is to say that experience shapes the way we believe. In the early church, this meant that the experience of worship was a priority. In the community of faith, one's behavior was influenced by the communal experience of worship.

Today, in the field of education, experts like Thomas Groome, author of *Christian Religious Education,* are in full agreement with the ancient principle of *lex orandi; lex credendi; est.* It is valued not only because it is a principle of education and formation found among biblical peoples, but because it is a principle demanded by the more dynamic view of the world which now prevails.

When *lex orandi; lex credendi; est.* is applied to worship, it is best stated as "worship is faith in motion." That is, the primary purpose of worship is not to provide discursive teaching about God, Christ, sin, salvation, the church, ethical behavior, and social concern. Instead, the primary purpose of worship is to experience faith in the community of worship in such a way that the Christian faith is not merely known intellectually, but experienced as a reality. In this kind of worship, the Christian faith is taught by being caught. Herein lies the key to aliveness in worship: a Spirit-filled congregation—a warm, loving, and caring community of people—is by its very existence a community of faith in motion. Such a congregation will so actualize the faith that if someone were to ask, "Where can I go to find God?," a person may answer, "Go to that church for God dwells in their worship." This is the kind of worship in which a person may establish, maintain, and repair a relationship with God.

I doubt that any church committed to the gospel would say, "I don't want that." I sense that nearly all pastors, music ministers, worship committee members, and lay people (who are themselves ministers) would say, "That's what I want—a worship where God touches people's lives in a very real way." So the question most congregations need to address is the issue of how—how can this kind of worship happen in our church? First of all, this "how to" question is not a matter of technique but an issue of being. Believers are called to be a worshiping community. The "how to" question is, however, best addressed in a discussion of three principles of worship: worship celebrates Christ; divine action occurs in worship; and we respond to God's action by faith with open hearts. Worship based on these principles is worship in which God can touch his people's lives with his transforming power.

Principles of the Sunday Morning Worship Experience

I have previously mentioned how worship celebrates the event of Christ's death and resurrection and the dethronement of the powers of evil. I now want to be more clear about how the Christ-event shapes contemporary worship.

Worship Celebrates Christ

I will begin by saying what I do not mean by Christocentric worship as a way of making more clear what I do mean. First, to say that worship celebrates Christ does not mean that worship is an evangelistic service. We associate evangelism with a Billy Graham crusade. In a crusade there are acts associated with worship such as singing, praying, and preaching. Nevertheless, evangelism is not worship because the thrust of the service is directed toward the people, particularly the sinner, with the intention of bringing the sinner to a personal relationship with God through Christ.

Unfortunately, many churches have brought this evangelistic model into the Sunday morning service and called it worship. It is not worship; it is evangelism. The church must be about evangelism, but it must also be about worship—and worship is not primarily directed toward the people. Rather, worship is the people's celebration of the living, dying, and rising of Christ, a celebration which is offered to God's glory. This is what the New Testament calls *leiturgia,* the work of the people.

The work of the people is to celebrate, and this work of the people is something the people experience. That is, they do it. It is not done to them or for them, but by them. And the planners of worship must be conscious of this. They must work to enable their people to do in worship what they are called to do: celebrate Christ by the power of the Spirit and to the glory of God.

This celebration of the living, dying, and rising of Christ occurs through the different elements of a worship service. Christ is to be experienced by the people from the beginning to the end of a worship service. This happens through song, prayer, Scripture, and the passing of the peace; in healing; and at the Table of the Lord. In worship, the Spirit brings Christ and delivers the benefit of Christ's death and resurrection through the words and symbols of worship.

While the experience of Christ in such infrastructure acts of worship as songs and prayers are important vehicles through which Christ is celebrated, the most important celebration of Christ will be in the broader structure of worship, namely in the Word and at the Table of the Lord. Christ is the central figure of the whole of Scripture. The Service of the Word, then, rightly proclaims Christ as the Lord over all dislocations of life. The Service of the Word also calls people to follow Christ's teaching and imitate his life. In the Eucharist, which is the church's thanksgiving, God's people offer praise and thanksgiving to the Father for the work of the Son through which salvation and healing come by the Spirit. In these acts, Christ is celebrated and, through the celebration, communicates himself to the worshipers.

Those people responsible for planning worship need to keep this Christocentric purpose of worship foremost in their minds. Planners must always ask: Does the content of worship adequately re-present Christ? Will the work of the people be a true celebration of the living, dying, rising, and coming again of Jesus Christ? Is the fact that Jesus Christ is Lord and Savior of all creatures and of the entire universe celebrated in worship?

In Worship There Is Divine Action

The second principle for true and lively worship is that in worship there is divine action. In our celebration of Christ, something happens. There is an action from above: the Holy Spirit delivers Christ and the benefits of Christ's death and resurrection to the worshipers.

In other words, in worship our relationship with Christ is established, maintained, and repaired. Christ meets us in our act of celebrating his death and resurrection. In this worship encounter, the Spirit brings us the very real benefits of Christ's death—salvation, healing, comfort, hope, guidance, and assurance. Through this encounter, order and meaning come into our lives. Through worship, a right ordering of God, the world, self, and neighbor is experienced, and the worshiper receives a peace that passes understanding. Simply put, worship is an it-is-well-with-my-soul experience.

Unfortunately, many people do not experience this kind of rest in worship. I have talked to people who experience boredom, anger, frustration, a stomach tied in knots, and even despair in their worship. Why? I am convinced that a worship directed to the people—that is, a worship that intends to teach, evangelize, or entertain—does not do what true worship does. True worship is never directed from the "platform" to the "audience" as is so much of our teaching, evangelizing, and entertaining. True worship happens among people who celebrate Christ. Jesus dwells in their worship, bringing to them what he did for them on the cross and in the Resurrection.

The Cross and the Resurrection—this is the constant theme of worship. And we find in Christ's dying and resurrection the pattern of our own life. Each of us knows the recurring experience of dying to sin and the powers of evil that would corrupt and distort our lives and then rising to the new life of the Spirit, a life of joy, peace, long-suffering, kindness, goodness, faithfulness, gentleness and self-control. But how does this happen? How does the benefit of the death and resurrection of Christ manifest our own dying to sin and rising to the newness of life? It happens by the power of the Spirit who works through the content of our worship. Christ comes to us in worship when, with a sense of expectancy, we recite and enact the reality of God acting in history for us. He then enters our worship to bring healing into our lives and to form us into his body, his presence in the world.

In the recitation and enactment of these saving deeds, our lives—our struggles, failures, hurts, successes, joys, and sorrows—are lifted up into God's saving action and given meaning through the incarnation of God in history and in our lives. We celebrate that God became one of us in order to experience life in the world and set us free by his death and resurrection. Because of his work, we no longer need to be slaves to those powers that would distort and demean our lives. Instead, we are now free to live in the newness of life. When we participate in Christ's resurrection through worship, we experience his transforming resurrection power.

The worshipers who experience most fully this transforming power are the poor, the oppressed, the needy, the destitute. These people bring their very real struggles to worship, and they find hope. This is why worship among the blacks and the poor in America and in developing countries is so often full of joy. In worship, the people experience a new reality. They are lifted out of their pain into a momentary experience of the future, into the new heavens and the new earth.

In worship, then, being wealthy and successful can, in a sense, be a disadvantage. What do people who have nice homes to live in, fancy cars to drive, delicious food to eat, and plenty of money in their pocket experience in worship? Theirs may be a poverty of spirit, or they may bring to worship the personal and family issues they are wrestling with. For the most part, though, I doubt that those who rest in their riches can have a worship experience as significant or meaningful as that of the common and poor folk of this world.

In worship, rich and poor alike recite God's actions in history and in our very lives through the songs, prayers, Scripture, sermon, and Eucharist. Like Psalm 136, worship has as its constant underlying theme the fact that the God who was present in the past is present now and will be in the future.

In worship, we need to recite and enact salvation history so that we can experience God's salvation in a personal way. The psalmist serves as a model. In many of those Old Testament songs, the psalmist begins with an account of his woes. Life is falling apart, and the psalmist doesn't mind saying so. But then the psalmist remembers how God has acted in the history of Israel and how he faithfully brought his people out of their plight. Then the psalmist realizes that this God who brought Israel out of its bondage will bring him out of his woes. The psalmist becomes aware of his own salvation and rejoices in God (see Psalm 40). This is exactly and ideally what believers can experience in worship. Worship is a divine action, a word from above that everything will be all right because God has acted in history and comes now in worship to save us, to form us, to heal us, to comfort us, and to give us hope.

Worship Necessitates a Human Response

By now it should be clear that the presence of God in worship—the divine action of God meeting with us in worship—calls for an open and total response from us. Worship calls for the involvement of our mind, body, and soul. Worship demands nothing less than the complete, conscious, and deliberate participation of the worshiper. Worship planners therefore need to provide open spaces for corporate response: dialogue, acclamations, proclamations, antiphonal response, and physical response are all vehicles through which a "yes" may be said to God's action in worship.

To summarize, meaningful worship is characterized by a three-way action. First, we celebrate the death and resurrection of Jesus Christ, offering praise and thanksgiving to the Father by the Spirit. Second, God dwells in that offering of praise, bringing to us the benefit of Christ for the maintenance, repair, and transformation of our relationship to God. Third, we receive God's transforming power by being open to the divine action and allowing the Spirit to mold us into the image of Christ. In this three-way action, the gospel is in motion, transforming the life of the worshiper and offering hope and renewal.

The Process of Worship

In order to plan worship in which God breaks into our lives with his transforming power, we must understand the process by which this happens. I want to first make it clear that the biblical and historical process of worship does not necessitate a particular type of worship (liturgical, traditional Protestant, creative, or praise and worship tradition). Nevertheless, some elements of biblical and historical worship—namely, the overall order and the underlying structure—ought to be found in every style of worship. The infrastructure of this order may vary from group to group as would the style, ranging from formal to informal.

The Common Order of Worship

Let me suggest that worship, which is fundamentally a meeting between God and his people, is analogous to what we do in everyday life as we meet with various people in both formal and informal settings. When we entertain friends in our home, for instance, we first take time to prepare. We purchase the food and carefully prepare it so it is pleasant to look at and delicious to taste. We clean the house, set the table, choose good music, start a fire in the fireplace, and generally concern ourselves with making our home conducive to an enjoyable evening with people we like.

When the guests arrive, we fling open the door, welcome our friends with open arms, and do various acts of verbal and symbolic greeting which express the joy of being together. Then we sit or walk around the house eating hors d'oeuvres and talking about family, friends, interests, and life in general. Someone finally says, "Dinner is ready. Let's gather at the table." At the table, we eat, we talk, and we laugh. We continue to engage in various verbal and symbolic acts that express the joy of being together and that deepen our relationships and our commitment to one another. Finally, the meal is over. We conclude the evening with words and gestures of departure, promising to see each other soon because the time together was so rich and rewarding.

Look again at the above description. It is easy to see that a normal meeting between friends consists of four acts: (1) acts which constitute the entrance; (2) acts of communication; (3) the act of eating; and (4) the act of dismissal. Herein lies a key to understanding the process of worship. What do we do when we come to worship

God? We (1) enter into God's presence; (2) communicate with God through the Word which we hear and to which we respond; (3) eat with Christ at the Table of the Lord; and (4) depart into the world to serve the Lord in our daily lives. Through these actions, a meeting takes place between God and his people, a meeting that enriches our relationship to God, a meeting that blesses us, encourages us, comforts us, and challenges us. In fact, the meeting is so powerful and significant for us that we want to do it again and again.

Conclusion

Finally, allow me to reflect on the way the three principles and the order of worship I have described accomplish a lively worship. And by "lively" I do not mean loud or bombastic; I mean real, authentic, engaging, and fulfilling.

First, the principles of worship (that worship celebrates Christ, a divine action occurs, and we respond) are rooted in the gospel. Scripture demands that we proclaim Christ boldly and energetically. It is here, in the coming together of God's actions and our response, that such aliveness occurs. Why? Because aliveness requires something to happen. We have been touched by and we've responded to God's transforming power—and our worship is alive.

Because of the availability of God's power in worship, good worship never covers up problems. Instead, living worship confronts evil in the overcoming name of Jesus. Good worship gives the worshiper permission to deal with his or her struggles and to bring them before God for healing. This openness results in the spiritual development of the worshiper as well as the transformation of the community of worshipers into the image of Christ.

Also, the process of worship is ultimately a rehearsal of our relationship to God. In worship, we come before God and hear him speak to our struggles. We once again experience the Good News that Christ is the victor. We offer praise and thanksgiving to God at the Table, a praise in which God dwells, and we leave to serve God in the newness of life.

I have found for myself that in this kind of worship God comes to us with his loving power. If we have space in our worship for divine action and human response, God is free to be there, to touch people where they hurt, and to give the church a vision of its own ministry of redemption in the world.

Bibliography

I have developed the principles of worship at length in my book *Worship Is a Verb* (Nashville: Abbott Martyn, 1992). Other books that touch on these principles, but not systematically, include Barry Liesch, *People in the Presence of God* (Grand Rapids: Zondervan, 1988); Ronald Allen and Gordon Borror, *Worship: Rediscovering the Missing Jewel* (Portland: Multnomah, 1982); and James F. White, *Introduction to Christian Worship* (Nashville: Abingdon, 1980).

For a more complete discussion of the four parts of worship, see Mark Searle, *Liturgy Made Simple* (Collegeville: The Liturgical Press, 1981) and *Companion to the Book of Resources* (Nashville: Abingdon Press, 1988).

For resources for each of the four parts of worship, see *The Book of Services* (Nashville: The United Methodist Publishing House, 1985); *The Service for the Lord's Day* (Philadelphia: The Westminster Press, 1984); and *Thankful Praise* (St. Louis: CBP Press, 1987).

7

---------------- ✧ ----------------

Encountering Christ
through the Arts

The worshiping church recognizes that God communicates through the arts and is therefore paying attention to environmental art, old and new styles of music, drama, and dance as the means by which Christ is encountered.

MOSCOW IS AN ENCHANTING CITY full of marvelous and beautiful centuries-old Orthodox churches. I'm told there are fourteen hundred churches in the city, and I believe it. At night the entire skyline seems ablaze with the sparkle of golden onion-shaped domes that rise high into the sky like shimmering hands lifted in open and joyful praise.

Trinity Sunday 1977 was a memorable day for me. I had arrived in Moscow earlier in the week and had already visited a number of historic churches. I had not yet attended an actual worship service.

On this day of the Trinity, my first Sunday in Moscow, I caught a cab at my hotel and was quickly transported down the broad streets of that beautiful city to my destination, the Church of the Holy Trinity. As we passed along those expansive boulevards, I was struck by the emptiness of the streets. Here, in one of the largest cities of the world, barely a car was in sight. And only here and there did I see a person or two huddled together waiting for a bus or walking the street while they fought the cold wind of the morning.

I soon arrived at the Church of the Holy Trinity in downtown Moscow. A few people were milling around outside, people I assumed were making their way to the service. I guessed there would be a few people inside, but not many. Maybe fifty or more women in their drab overcoats with babushkas tied around their heads.

I walked up to the huge wooden door of this many-domed cathedral and pulled it open to find I was among a group of people standing against the door. Just a few latecomers, I thought. But then my eyes rose above their heads. As far as I could see to the front, to the right, and to the left, people were jammed shoulder to shoulder (there are no pews in Orthodox churches in Russia).

I was soon greeted by a woman who spoke to me through my companion, an Australian translator. When she found out I was an American Christian, she seemed overwhelmed with joy for my presence. Fortunately for us, she was able to push through the worshipers (they do that in Russia) and take us near the front of the church. There we were able to see the people in action and feel and experience the worship in that place.

I was deeply moved by the worship of the people. I always find myself moved by the heartfelt worship of other people, and this situation was no exception. These people were busy at worship, lost in participation, a participation I have seldom experienced anywhere else. These people were in heaven standing around the throne of God, singing, praying, and moving with the angels, archangels, cherubim, and seraphim. Faces were lifted upward, eyes closed, lips moving, hands doing the sign of the Cross.

I was stunned. I've been in many American churches where worship is reduced to an intellectual experience, where visible signs of worship such as closed eyes, tears, or expressive hands are seldom seen. But here I was in an Orthodox church where the intensity of emotion and feeling reminded me of my experiences in many praise and worship tradition churches. These people—old and young alike—were lost in wonder and praise.

I began looking at my surroundings—at the people, the space, the walls, the ceiling, and the iconostasis screen. Here, in various icons and frescoes, was the entire company of saints. Christ was in the dome ruling over the heavens with all the saints who had gone before: Abraham, Moses, David, Isaiah, Hosea, Daniel, the Twelve Apostles, Mary the Mother of Jesus, Mary Magdalene, Lazarus, and many more of God's people now in the heavens.

Something was very different. I had seen all these icons and frescoes before, but this was my first time to see them as I worshiped. I felt as though I, even I, was joining with the heavenly company of saints, that together with them I was lifting my heart and voice in praise to God.

This was a pivotal experience for me: it left me very aware of the importance of the environment in which we worship, a matter which all renewing congregations must attend to. While I am not advocating icons and frescoes in Protestant churches, I am at least arguing against inattention to the space in which we worship and for a return of the arts to their rightful place in worship. Let me give you an example.

Crescent Hill Baptist Church is a large Southern Baptist church located near Southern Theological Seminary in Louisville, Kentucky. I had heard about their unusual commitment to the arts through my friend Dr. Donald Hustad, so I flew to Kentucky to worship with this congregation and to talk with their pastor Dr. Steven Shoemaker.

As I was making my way up the back steps to the sanctuary, I was greeted by an attractively appointed banner that welcomed me with the word "REJOICE!" I needed to see that word because I had been traveling for a succession of weekends, was worn out physically, and was wondering whether or not this trip was going to be worth it.

I thanked God for that word of welcome and made my way into the spacious sanctuary complete with a balcony on both sides. Even before I sat down, I was struck by the "Passion Collage" atop the large Communion table which stood in front of the pulpit on a raised platform. I sat closely enough so I could see the objects. The Table was covered with a purple cloth (the color of Lent), and a rose-colored runner crossed the middle of the table (a symbol of hope).

I began to study the stunning display by artist Dwight Cobb, and I soon found that I had entered into prayer. Here were all the signs and symbols of the events surrounding the death and resurrection of our Lord, the event for which we prepare during the season of Lent.

On the left side of the table, perched against an earth-toned water pot from the first century, was a striking crown of thorns with its ugly and cruel thorns quite visible. In front of the crown of thorns were several large, cruel-looking spikes and, to the right, a money bag for the thirty pieces of silver. To the right of these symbols of the Passion stood a striking bowl of fresh green and red grapes. Slightly to the right but a little behind them was a chalice and, in front of that, a freshly baked loaf of bread on a patent. A small pitcher for the wine stood nearby. To the far right was a basin for washing feet. Behind the basin was a large earthen pitcher with a towel draped over the handle. To the left of the water vessel, behind all the other objects, were stalks of wheat, palm branches, and a long stick with hyssop on the end.

Here I was on the second Sunday of Lent, a long way from home and among a thousand people I did not know. But there in front of me were all the visual symbols that unite black and white, male and female, children and retirees, liturgical and nonliturgical people. Before my eyes, the entire Passion was brought to me, and I encountered Jesus. There was the Jesus who washed the feet of the disciples, instituted the Lord's Supper, was betrayed for thirty pieces of silver, was nailed to the cross, and was offered vinegar to drink when he was thirsty. This was the Jesus who died for me and took my place on the cross, and here I was present to all of these saving events simultaneously because an artist cared to minister to me visually. Through the gifts God had given, the artist was communicating the most important event in human history. I was not only ready for worship, but I had already been worshiping! Now I was eager to offer my God my praise and thanksgiving even with this community of people I did not know.

After a few announcements and an introduction, the service began with a full procession. Two purple banners led the way. The choir, worship leaders, and pastor followed wearing gowns with purple appointments to indicate the season of Lent.

The two large banners that led the procession were crucial to the service. They bore the theme of the day, a Lenten theme: "Buried with Christ in baptism. . . . Raised to walk in newness of life." The banners were simple and striking as they boldly proclaimed their message. After the procession, the banners were hung from the balcony in full view of all who worshiped. I looked first at the banner to the left, bearing the message "Buried with Christ in baptism," and then to the banner on the right with its image of running water. These banners drew me into the spirit of Lent which has as its dominant image our baptism and death in Christ. The banners spoke to me, calling me into a remembrance of my baptismal vows. I quietly reflected on my life and on my calling, as a baptized person, to always live in the waters of my baptism into Christ.

My senses were involved in worship once again through a dramatic interpretation of the Scripture, the story of the conversion of Nicodemus in John 2:23-3:15. A member of the church, Janet Rittenhouse, had written a poetic account of being born again, an account interpreted by Beth Blovin, Amy Carter, and Peggy Hester through drama and dance. The Nicodemus figure walked quietly to the Table of the Lord and sat on a step. The narrator read, "Then send your Spirit, God" as Nicodemus, now standing, raised his arms heavenward. The narrator continued, "Embrace me now as in my mother's womb. Plunge me into the depths of re-creation that I may emerge wholly different." During these lines, two figures surrounded Nicodemus with a strikingly beautiful lame cloth of an iridescent fuchsia color. The cloth prominently displayed the dove at the upper end, and streamers of peacock, royal blue, and silver flowed under the dove to the end of the cloth. Nicodemus disappeared into the cloth and, as the narrator read, "Let the buoyancy of your Spirit lift my soul back to the light, leaving my sins to be dispersed by eddies of joy," Nicodemus jumped from behind the cloth as though to stand in the newness of life.

The narrator continued, "Once in the light, will it dry the drops of water, will the wind parch me as before?" As the fabric was brought close to the body of Nicodemus, the narrator said, "O God, tell me that the water is in me, to bubble forth. Let the wind be your Spirit, whispering to me of your love." The fabric surrounded the head of Nicodemus, showing that he was listening. The narrator continued:

" 'Even so,' says the Spirit, quenching my old nature, refreshing me, even setting me free. And in the Spirit's voice I hear my own laughter for I called out for my God and found you, Abba.'" As these striking words were read, the fabric was released from around Nicodemus, the dove was displayed in full, and Nicodemus, now reborn, again threw his hands upward, this time as a sign of the new person.

In these words and actions, my own experience of being made anew in Christ was rehearsed. The dramatization of the Nicodemus story compelled me to continue to rise to the calling of my newness in Christ Jesus.

The concept of the arts now, as in the days of the early church, is rooted in an understanding of the implications of the Incarnation, implications which too many people readily ignore. A theology of the Incarnation says that God, the immaterial one, became present in this created world in a material, tangible way. What this means for the arts is that the divine chooses to become present through creation, through wood, stone, mortar, color, sound, shape, form, movement, and action. Christians are not Gnostics. We do not reject the body, the material, the tangible. To do so would be to reject the Incarnation. We affirm the created order because God himself took on the creation in the Incarnation. Therefore, we need to set the creation free to bespeak redemption through the use of the arts in worship.

The arts are important not only because of the Incarnation, but also because they communicate. The arts are the language of the intuition, a poetic, imaginative way of supporting and enhancing the text of worship, the gospel. I sense that much of our Protestant worship is suffering from verbal overdose. We feel the need to explain everything as though verbal communication is the only legitimate form of communication. We need to learn to trust the arts, to see, touch, smell, and hear what they have to say. The arts are an active symbol, a visible word, a visual speech. They can and do speak. They can be used by the Spirit to communicate. But we have to learn to hear what the arts are saying, to befriend them, to let them live among us, worship with us, and serve as a vehicle for our praise.

Renewing churches like Crescent Hill Baptist are rediscovering the significance of the arts for their worship. Wherever I travel, I find new attention to environmental art, music, drama, and liturgical dance, what some call "praise in motion."

Environmental Art

Environmental art is, first and foremost, the space in which we worship and, second, the furniture, hangings, and symbols with which we fill it. And this environment can indeed enhance and enliven the worship experience.

There is a saying attributed to Frank Lloyd Wright: "We shape our environment and then our environment shapes us." I think this is particularly true in worship. I recall one growing church that first met in a very small space where people were close together. The space generated a feeling of warmth, hospitality, and community. But then the church built a much larger space that distanced the people from each other and from the action of worship. Soon the people who had once shared a sense of community began to reflect the coldness and distance of their worship space. This correlation between space and the hospitality of the people who worship there does indeed seem inextricably bound together. A church that meets in a cold and uninviting space yet maintains a warm and hospitable community feeling is rare. Space speaks. It is a visible word, a form of communication that speaks to us in subliminal ways.

Marshall McLuhan is famous for saying, "The medium is the message." This truth is expressed in a building that is being planned by Irvine Presbyterian Church in Irvine, California. Before planning their new sanctuary, the building committee asked me to spend a weekend lecturing on the theology of worship and space. They wanted to know, "What does worship do?" as a way of dealing with, "What do we want our space to say?" Like McLuhan, they were convinced that the medium in which worship is done needs to support the action of worship, not fight it.

Unfortunately, the space in many churches works against worship renewal because the space is designed for worship that is either evangelistic or given to lecture style. For this reason, many Protestant churches have a front "stage" or "platform" with a pulpit, three chairs, a choir behind, a piano to the left, and an organ to the right. This space is good for listening and watching, but it does not support the current recovery of a worship that is dialogic and participatory.

Irvine Presbyterian Church turned its back on an evangelistic, Enlightenment, or entertainment space and designed a space for worship that fits our participatory age, a space that sets people free to worship together. The building committee planned their worship space around three themes—God's being, God's works, and God's people—and wrote a paper explaining the theology of space to the congregation. God's works, the committee's paper pointed out, are creation, redemption, and eschaton. The conviction that creation glorifies the Lord and proclaims his splendor and power led them to feature natural materials: natural light and living plants would remind the worshiper that the whole universe is the sanctuary of the living God.

The paper continued: Because Scripture reading, preaching, and the sacraments proclaim God's acts of salvation, "the furniture and fixtures relating to the preaching of the Word and the administration of the sacraments must be imbued with gained significance and occupy a place of prominence in the chancel." And because the eschaton is the promise that one day earthly worship will be joined with heavenly worship, the sanctuary, they wrote, "needs to express the glory of the kingdom, the unity of the church in heaven and earth, and the hope of eternal life."

Finally, the committee turned its attention to the space for the people, the community of worship. Because this is a "house of worship," they wrote, the space should not resemble "a lecture hall or auditorium" but should "foster a mood of prayerfulness and meditation rather than one of chattering conviviality." Consequently, "the seating will be gently arched so that we are aware of each other's presence, but not so much that we are distracted from worship." And because we gather in community to serve others, "our sanctuary should inspire us to live our lives in service to the Lord."

Not all churches which seek worship renewal have the luxury of building a new space. Nevertheless, attention needs to be given to the existing space. How can the space be modified so that it works for worship renewal and not against it? Many churches have refurbished their space by rearranging the seating in a semicircle, by placing both table and pulpit in prominent places, and by using appropriately placed banners, wall hangings, or Christian symbols. These touches add a sense of being connected with God's whole church as well as a feeling of warmth and hospitality.

Ultimately, a church has to wrestle with the relationship between space and its understanding of worship. Space does communicate. It can communicate warmth, hospitality, awe, reverence, and remembrance of God's action in history. Space can also evoke praise, worship, silence, and hope. There is no single correct or effective style. All these emotions can be evoked in a stately cathedral or in a building that is quite contemporary. It is important for a renewing church to pay attention to how God encounters us through space and to become intentional in the way it uses space for worship.

Music

Once we have created the space in which we worship, we are to fill it with the text of worship and with those sounds, actions, and movements which speak of our encounter with God. While it is possible to worship without the arts, modern worshipers are acutely aware of how important the arts are to worship. The arts are the wheels upon which the text of worship moves. They lift worship from an enslavement to words and set worship free to happen through action and symbolism.

A great deal is happening in music and worship today. Space does not permit the exploration of the shift from choir to cantor, a study of the various genres of music, or a discussion of the return of hymn festivals, the restoration of psalm singing, the emergence of a new hymnology, the restoration of ancient hymns, the birth of new praise choruses, or the use of Taize music. I will concentrate, therefore, on two matters: the mixing of musical styles in worship and the conviction that music must serve the text of worship, not dominate it.

First, the trend to mix music styles is a phenomenon found all over the world. What I mean by the mixing of musical styles is that renewing churches are becoming aware of styles of music from other traditions and discovering how their worship is enriched by music from other traditions and cultures. For example, we usually associate stately hymns with liturgical churches. But I have been in Catholic, Orthodox, Anglican, and Lutheran churches where the contemporary choruses we usually associate with the praise and worship tradition have been sung in worship, especially at Communion.

I visited an Orthodox worship service for the first time about twenty years ago when the praise chorus was first being introduced by the Jesus people. This orthodox worship, which was in both English and Slavic, was the ancient John Chrysostom service written in A.D. 380. According to the ancient custom, we sang through that whole service in three parts: the priest, the choir, and the congregation each had its own part. I was drawn up into this ancient way of singing without musical instruments and according to various sprightly tones. The tones evoked awe, majesty, and mystery. The sounds themselves lifted me up into the heavens. But when it came time to receive the bread and wine mixed together in a single cup— the tradition of the East—I was startled to hear, "Seek ye first the kingdom of God—and all these things shall be added unto you." I have experienced the same blending of worship traditions in other Orthodox churches and in many Episcopal and Lutheran churches as well.

At the same time, I have found that charismatics and praise and worship tradition people are beginning to discover the ancient hymn as well as some of the new hymns that are currently being introduced into worship. I recently spoke to a charismatic pastor who said, "There are many of us who are now trying to figure out how to bring the traditional back into our worship." Although he was referring to more than music, he made a specific comment about the need to reclaim the great hymns of the past.

Perhaps this is partly the influence of Jack Hayford, well-known pastor of the Church on the Way in Van Nuys, California, and writer of many songs including the popular "Majesty." Pastor Hayford always has his congregation sing at least one historic hymn in worship.

As renewing churches learn to mix musical styles effectively, they also need to find a way to use music in worship so that music serves the text rather than dominates it. I recently attended a charismatic church given to singing only choruses to the accompaniment of a loud band complete with drum set and crashing cymbals. During worship, a time was given for chorus singing alone, and chorus singing was scattered throughout the various other parts of worship. I came away from that service with an unsettled feeling, a feeling that I needed to identify and analyze for myself and for those who are committed to a steady diet of praise music.

At lunch with friends from that church, I began to talk about my feelings with the hope that I might gain some clarity about my own experience. What emerged from that conversation were three insights which I've since shared with other people from the praise tradition. I've found that they feel somewhat the same way but had not been able to articulate it. First, I sensed that the steady diet of choruses became tiring. There were spaces in the worship where I wanted a change of pace, more substance to my song, some quietness. I felt I was kept in a constant state of enthusiasm, that the continuous use of the same rhythm and same style of praise became somewhat trite, and that I simply wanted all the noise to stop for a while and give me a chance to be quiet before the Lord.

Second, I felt that the service was dominated by choruses which overshadowed the text. At lunch I referred to it as a "chorus-driven service, not a text-driven service." The text of worship actually became a footnote to the songs. What kept that worship together from beginning to end was not the text of the gospel in motion, but the sameness of the musical beat, the overwhelming noise of the band, and the similarity of the musical content.

And, third, I felt that the music often clashed with the action of the text. Even when the text of the service called for solemnity, repentance, or silence, the music was always there, clashing with the text and sending the sensitive worshiper in two different directions. The text might have been saying, "Pray and be quiet." But the music was saying, "Get up, rejoice, be glad, and dance!" Somehow music must serve the text, not dominate it or fight it.

I experienced how music can effectively serve the text of the Entrance at St. Bartholomew's Episcopal Church in Nashville, Tennessee, a church that seeks to blend both ancient hymnody and contemporary praise music. The purpose of the Entrance is to bring us into the presence of God and ready us to hear the Word of the Lord. Here is how text and music were combined to enhance our entrance into the presence of God:

Opening Words of Praise:
Celebrant: Blessed be God: Father, Son, and
                         Holy Spirit
People: And blessed be his kingdom now
                         and forever. Amen.
Collect for Purity:
Celebrant and People: Almighty God, to you all hearts are open, all desires known, and from you no secrets are hid. Cleanse the thoughts of our hearts by the inspiration of your Holy Spirit that we may perfectly love you and worthily magnify your holy name; through Christ our Lord. Amen.
PROCESSIONAL HYMN   "Immortal, Invisible"
PRAISE MUSIC   "Majesty"
                                "You Are the
                                  Mighty King"
Collect for the Day (all in unison): O God, the strength of all who put their trust in you: mercifully accept our prayers; and because in our weakness we can do nothing good without you, give us the help of your grace, that in keeping your commandments we may please you both in will and deed; through Jesus Christ our Lord, who lives and reigns with you and the Holy Spirit, one God, forever and ever. Amen.

Renewing churches will have to commit to constant attention to their worship until each congregation finds a way to bring together the varieties of music in a way that serves the text of worship. In the above example, the music of the Entrance serves the joyful note of the text. In the Service of the Word, music should be more quiet and pensive, serving the mood of learning. In the Service of the Table, music and text bring us through the death of Christ and into Resurrection joy. And finally, in the Dismissal, music sends us forth into the world with a sense of our calling to worship through our life and work.

Drama

Several years ago I was invited to speak at a worship congress held at the Billy Graham Center in Wheaton. Our agenda was to worship in the style of various worshiping communities and then discuss our experience. One of the churches participating was the Christian Missionary Alliance Church of Wheaton, a church known for its use of drama.

They chose to dramatize the passage of Scripture in which the woman taken in adultery was brought to Jesus. In a burst of excitement, the woman was forcibly brought to the front by a man accusing her of sin. Three more accusers followed, each carrying a large stone. The figure of Jesus looked on silently, dropped to his knees, wrote in the sand, then rose and looked at the accusers who were standing there with raised arms ready to throw the stones. In a quiet but strong voice, the Jesus figure said, "He who is without sin, let him cast the first stone." A provocative silence followed, and I looked at one accuser and then another. Eyes dropped and arms holding stones were slowly lowered. The accusers turned away from Jesus, each recognizing that "I, too, am a sinner." I saw myself in these accusers, these would-be stone throwers; with them I dropped the stones in my hands and lowered my arms which had been poised against those whom I would judge. And when I heard those words, "Go and sin no more," they were spoken to me, a sinner always in need of God's grace.

We need to remember that worship itself is a kind of drama. Like drama, worship has a script. And, like drama, the script has to be learned. I remember how I felt in college when we met for the first several times to talk about and read through a script. (I was a speech and drama major.) The play always seemed dead and lifeless. Once we were free of reading the text and, especially, after we had memorized it and become the character we played, the drama took on a life of its own and leaped to a new level of excitement and communication. Experiences like that have convinced me that we need to learn the script of worship. Learning the script sets us free to enter into the drama and play our part with full attention to the meaning of our praise and worship. I suggest that people in liturgical churches study and then memorize their worship and that people in nonliturgical churches at least be aware of the underlying script and movement of their worship.

Because worship is a drama which acts out our relationship to God, both what God has done for us in Christ and our response to that action, I'm not at all convinced of the value of "doing something different" every Sunday. I cringe when I hear people brag, "You never know what to expect at our church. It's something new every Sunday." I think a congregation is much better off developing a script everyone knows—a script related to the four parts of worship discussed in the previous chapter—and using that script with some variation from Sunday to Sunday. The music, hymns, songs, and choruses as well as Scripture texts, the inclusion of drama or dance, and some environmental arts may change from Sunday to Sunday, but these are the parts of the drama that support the text, not the text itself. When the people have really learned the drama and know their parts, worship will be much more participatory and expressive than it would be if there is a new drama every week.

The only way a new drama can be sustained week after week is if the church opts for the entertainment model of worship. But this model is not biblical, and eventually the people will tire of merely being entertained. But when the people do the drama of worship themselves, they will return because they have been involved in the action of praising God, an action which is both biblical and personally satisfying.

Dance

For many people, dance in worship is a hot topic. Some think it belongs in worship; others do not.

Not long ago I did a workshop at Hillcrest Covenant Church in Kansas City that was attended by people from a number of different denominations. At the concluding service, a group of people did a ring dance around the Communion table to the Taize song "Gloria, Gloria, in Excelsis Deo, Gloria, Gloria, Halleluia! Halleluia!"

During the question-and-answer time, a woman, enraged by the dance, stood to her feet and, in a loud and judgmental voice, cried, "Tell me why you are bringing the barroom into the church and desecrating God's house!"

I must admit I was somewhat thrown by her question and especially by the tone of her voice. I managed to remain calm and explained to her how, in Christ, God had redeemed the entire creation—including movement—so that our praise of God could be in motion as well as in voice or lifted hand. Although she did not seem open to my answer, I sensed that other people knew what I was talking about and were quite supportive.

Dance, like music, art, or drama, must serve the text and never dominate it. Like the other arts, it should never be a performance, but a visual and physical expression of the text it accompanies. At Hillcrest Covenant Church, the text was the joy of the Resurrection, and the ring dance was simply an expression in movement of that joy.

A while back, I did a weekend retreat for the leaders of the Church of the Brethren in Illinois in which we addressed the propriety of dance in worship. One of the attendees was a woman who quite excelled at being able to express ideas through movement. I asked her to do a dance for us at the bringing of bread and wine to the Communion table, what is usually called the Offertory. Her movement was to the song "Break Thou the Bread of Life." Although this song was originally meant for the preaching of the Word, it can be used effectively at the bringing of the bread and wine. While we sang, she served the text: she provided hand and body motions that effectively portrayed the bringing and the breaking of the body. What was important about this dance is that it allowed me to visualize and feel the Word; her dance expressed what we were about to do. She did what dance and any art should do in worship—she served the text. Through the medium of movement, she allowed me to participate in the meaning of Communion in a way that went beyond the limitations of the verbal text.

Another kind of dance has been introduced by many charismatics, and that is the dance of joy, a participatory dance engaged in by the whole congregation. Recently in the chapel of Wheaton College during International Week, a group of Africans was in charge of the music. Africans love to dance in worship (sometimes for an hour or more), so these Africans decided they were going to lead the entire student body in song and dance. That's not an easy thing to do in Edman Chapel because the seats are fixed (another point to be aware of in planning worship space). Nevertheless, the worship leaders had all the students stand, and they taught them an African song with movement. I can't remember a more joyful experience in Edman Chapel! All day long the students were full of smiles, and they kept commenting on how freeing it was to dance to the Lord. My own experience concurs with theirs: dance is a way of expressing and feeling great joy in worship. And that is what worship is all about—a response of joy to God who through Jesus Christ has redeemed us and set us free.

Conclusion

Renewing churches are rediscovering the arts and their significance for worship. I have left much unsaid in this chapter on the arts in worship—I've said nothing about banners, textiles, pottery, sculpture, vestments, artistically adorned Bibles, candles, colors, musical instruments, and other matters pertinent to worship.

Instead, what I have argued is that renewing churches are paying attention to the arts, recognizing that worship itself is an art, and integrating the arts in worship. And the churches most sensitive to the arts are churches that give the arts a servant role in worship. Worship is never to be arts-driven, but arts-enhanced. What should be prominent in worship is the celebration of God's great deed of salvation in Jesus Christ. When the arts serve this message, they serve and assist our worship. Through the arts, then, our worship finds new dimensions of praise and thanksgiving. God dwells in the arts and becomes present to his people in a healing and comforting way as the arts bespeak redemption.

Bibliography

For a good survey of music throughout the history of the church, see Donald Hustad, *Jubilate* (Carol Stream: Hope Publishing Co., 1981). For an introduction to the use of music, see Marion G. Hatchett, *A Manual for Clergy and Church Musicians* (New York: The Church Hymnal Corporation, 1980); Joy E. Lawrence and John A. Ferguson, *A Musician's Guide to Church Music* (New York: The Pilgrim Press, 1981); and Paul Westermeyer, *The Church Musician* (New York: Harper & Row, 1988).

For environmental art, see James F. White and Susan J. White,

Church Architecture: Building and Renovating for Christian Worship (Nashville: Abingdon Press, 1988); Richard Vosko, *Through the Eye of a Rose Window: A Perspective on the Environment of Worship* (Saratoga, Calif.: Resource Publications, Inc., 1981); and Bernadette McCarver Snyder and Hazelmai McCarver Terry, *Decorating for Sundays and Holy Days* (Mystic, Conn.: Twenty-Third Publication, 1988).

Banner-making is made simple with Janet Litherland, *The Complete Banner Handbook: A Creative Guide for Banner Design and Construction* (Colorado Springs: Meriwhether Publishing LTD, 1987) and Jill Knott, *Banners without Words* (San Jose: Resource Publications, 1986).

To start a drama ministry, read Janet Litherland, *Getting Started in Drama Ministry* (Colorado Springs: Meriwhether Publishing LTD, 1988) and Judy Gattis Smith, *Drama through the Church Year* (Colorado Springs: Meriwhether LTD, 1984).

For liturgical dance, see Carol Deitering, *The Liturgy As Dance and the Liturgical Dancer* (New York: Crossroad, 1984); Marilyn Daniels, *The Dance in Christianity: A History of Religious Dance through the Ages* (New York: Paulist Press, 1981); Doug Adams and Diane Apostolas-Cappadona, *Dance As Religious Studies* (New York: Crossroad, 1990); and Ronald Gagne, Thomas Kane, Robert VerEcke, *Introducing Dance in Christian Worship* (Washington, D.C.: The Pastoral Press, 1984).

8

✧

Enacting Christ in the Services of the Christian Year

The worshiping church recognizes the evangelical nature of the Christian year and seeks to proclaim Christ effectively through celebrations of Advent, Christmas, Epiphany, Lent, Holy Week, Easter, and Pentecost.

I DO A CONSIDERABLE AMOUNT of speaking on worship among a variety of different Christian churches ranging from liturgical to praise tradition. Although I feel comfortable in all of these situations, I'm not always certain what to expect from place to place. . . .

About ten years ago I was speaking to a Presbyterian group at a time in my life when I was heavily involved in the study of the Christian year. On this particular occasion, I tackled the secular view of time which a number of churches have adopted. "Why," I asked, "have so many churches allowed the secular calendar to creep into their worship?" Instead of celebrating Christ, which is what worship is all about, the churches I was referring to celebrate national holidays, Mother's Day, Boy Scout Day, Girl Scout Day, and even Children's Day. "How much farther removed can you get," I challenged them, "from the real meaning of worship which focuses on the death and resurrection of Christ?"

I usually sense what my audience is feeling, and on this day I felt more hostility than usual. No one was laughing at my sarcasm about conservative churches opposing secular humanism at the same time they themselves are thoroughly secular at least in the matter of time. Instead, this large adult class sat there sipping coffee and staring at me as though I had just landed from another planet. When the bell rang to end class, they all filed out without so much as a glance toward me, let alone a friendly handshake or a "thank you for coming to speak to us" comment.

I knew I had offended them, but I wasn't aware of why or how deeply until I walked into the sanctuary and discovered to my chagrin that it was Boy Scout Sunday. There they were in the first several rows—fifty or more squirming adolescents all dressed up in their Boy Scout uniforms. Most of them were probably sons of the people I had just taught—or tried to teach.

If that church were to invite me back today—and they haven't and they probably won't—I'd tell them the same thing. We Protestants have secularized our time; we have allowed a secular view of time to permeate the worship of the church. What's worse, many Protestants seem proud to have escaped the Christian year. For them, it is a mark of spirituality to have rejected the church year which, after all, is Catholic and thanks be to God we were all saved from that by the Protestant Reformers. What's more, these purists proclaim, the dead Christians who follow the church year are nothing but liberal ritualists anyway. They have the form of godliness, but no power. It is of course true that, if misused, the services of the Christian year can become mere ritual, a form of godliness without power.

Nevertheless, I am thoroughly convinced of the evangelical nature of the church year and of its power to ignite a genuine Christian experience. This is already happening in nonliturgical churches all over the world, and many liturgical churches that were once ritualistic about the church year are rediscovering the power of the gospel unleashed by an evangelical practice of the church year. This rediscovery of the evangelical nature of the church year is a vital aspect of worship renewal today and cannot be ignored by those who would renew their worship.

The Evangelical Meaning of the Church Year

Throughout this book, I have presented the definition of worship as a celebration of the death and resurrection of Christ. It doesn't take a great deal of theological acumen to see how the Christian year is related to the death and resurrection of Christ, what the early Christians called the Paschal event.

In his first letter to the Corinthians, for instance, Paul challenges them to "get rid of the old yeast that you may be a new batch without yeast—as you really are. For Christ, our Passover lamb, has been sacrificed. Therefore let us keep the Festival, not with the old yeast, the yeast of malice and wickedness, but with the bread without yeast, the bread of sincerity and truth" (1 Corinthians 5:7-8 NIV). Every Sunday when Christians gather to worship, they celebrate the Christian Passover, but this Christian Passover also spans the entire year as an elongated feast, a continuous celebration of God's saving deeds in Jesus Christ.

We may look at the services of the Christian year this way: The salvation and healing of God's creatures and the world is brought about by the coming, living, dying, rising, ascending, and soon-to-come Christ. Salvation is historical. It arises from specific events, not some non-historical transaction that takes place outside of time, space, and history. God's work of salvation is in history and through history and will be accomplished within history. And the services of the Christian year cycle us through the experience of those salvation events annually.

Here lies the evangelical nature of the Christian year: the gospel events—events that took place in time, space, and history—find a tangible place in present time. And through this yearly rehearsal of the salvation events, our spirituality, insofar as we allow, is actually shaped by the story of salvation.

The story of salvation is a story of birth, life, death, resurrection, and empowerment. In the services of the church year, we celebrate this pattern of life, and we do so in such a way that our own birth and living, our own pattern of death (brokenness and failure) and resurrection (being raised to new life), and our own Pentecost (empowerment to live in the Spirit) are all lifted up into the pattern of the life and death of Jesus. By celebrating his life, death, and resurrection, we are constantly challenged into the newness of our own lives patterned on his death and resurrection.

Here is how it happens: Advent, when we wait for the coming of the Messiah, becomes our own spiritual waiting for the coming of Christ into our own lives; Christmas, which celebrates the birth of the Savior, becomes our own experience of Christ born within us; and Epiphany, which rejoices in the proclamation of God's salvation in Christ to the Gentile world (as to the Three Wise Men), becomes our own experience of recognizing Christ. Lent, which recalls the rising up against Jesus and the gathering storm that led to his rejection by his own people, becomes a journey into our own sin and rebellion against Christ and a call to renewal. Holy Week, which marches through the last days of Jesus from his triumphant entry on Palm Sunday to his crucifixion, death, and burial, becomes a representation of our own death to sin. Easter, the great resurrection of our Lord to newness of life, becomes our own resurrection, our new birth. Finally, Pentecost, the celebration of the coming of the Spirit, marks a new gift of the Spirit in our own lives.

I am convinced, not only by theology but by my own experience and that of others, that the restoration of the services of the Christian year are vital to the renewing of our worship. They guide us into an experience of Christ that, if done properly and in faith, can direct our spiritual pilgrimage into an ever-deepening relationship with him. The services of the Christian year also constantly remind us of God's saving deed and provide opportunities for him to touch us with his transforming power.

The Cycle of Light

In the Christian year, the Cycle of Light consists of Advent, Christmas, and Epiphany. These seasons are called the Cycle of Light because they celebrate the coming of the light of Christ to dispel the darkness of the world and the manifestation of the light of Christ to the whole world. Let me describe these services and the impact they make on our spirituality.

Advent

On the first Sunday of Advent in 1989, I was in Kansas City at Hillcrest Covenant Church, a church committed to worship renewal. In the large sanctuary, worshipers sit in a semicircle around a slightly raised platform on which the Table of the Lord and a pulpit are appropriately visible. On this Sunday, the church was not yet fully decorated for Advent as the greening of the church was to be held that night. Nevertheless, several signs of the season were already in place, notably the Advent wreath placed at the front of the sanctuary for all to see.

While the origins of the Advent wreath are unknown, the use of the wreath in Advent is a tradition that goes back to the medieval period. Now, as then, it is used to symbolize the coming of Christ. Like all Advent wreaths, the one at Hillcrest Covenant had five candles, four in an outer circle and one within the circle. The outer four represent the traditional four weeks of Advent which anticipate the coming of Christ, and the center one represents Christ. One candle is lighted each Sunday of Advent, and on Christmas Day the center candle is lighted as well. When all are lighted and burning brightly, they represent the birth of the one for whom the world has been waiting.

The first of these candles was lighted by a family whose members then read Scripture expressing the church's longing for Christ to come. Through the candle, the Scripture, and the prayer, I sensed the light that was to burn in my own heart for the season. With the lighting of the Advent candle, I entered into the spiritual experience of waiting for the Messiah, of preparing for the birth of Christ within me. Then, as we joined with the spirit of the upward flame of the candle in singing "Come Thou Long Expected Jesus," I sensed we were joining in Israel's wait. That Advent hope born within me was intensified.

This visual manifestation of the coming of Christ is a significant part of Advent. It shifts the tone of the season before Christmas away from the crass secular materialism of our age and calls us to focus on the true meaning of Christmas. Advent helps us keep looking ahead to the birth of the one who will go to the cross and then emerge from the tomb to resurrect us and this world to a newness of life.

For our own spiritual health, Advent should be a time of waiting, a time of preparing for God to break into our lives with his transforming power. Advent means "God comes," but some Christians do not even feel the need for God. Their lives are "together." They do not face sickness, hunger, oppression, or loss. All is going well—or at least seems to be. These people have become desensitized to their own situation and to the pains and struggles of most people in the world. Advent is a time when the church, through the themes of the season, can help these Christians get in touch with a sense of the very real need in their own lives—and in the life of the world— for an in-breaking of God. Those who suffer from financial difficulties, the failure of a marriage, or a life-threatening disease and those who live in perpetual hunger or oppression and already long for God to break into their lives will find that Advent worship clarifies their longing and articulates their hope.

Christmas

For me, one of the most significant joys of participating in the church year is the traditional Christmas Eve service, a service that begins on Christmas Eve and ends at 1:00 a.m. on the day of the birth of Jesus. This service, or an adaptation of it, is being restored in many churches as the renewal of worship extends to the observance of the Christian year.

I never travel over Christmas, so I always have the privilege of being at my own church for the Christmas Eve service. Although St. Mark's Episcopal Church meets in a new building, it is a sanctuary that brings together the old and the new. The walls are white, a striking contrast to the stained wood ceilings that vault into the air as if to carry the praise and worship of the people heavenward. In front, above the pulpit and table and stained in the same color as the pews, is a large and striking Jerusalem cross that speaks of both the suffering and the resurrection of our Lord. On Christmas Eve, I see the "light" side of the cross, the light of the one who comes in the name of the Lord, the one who is God with us, Emmanuel.

At St. Mark's, the Christmas Eve service joyously begins with a thirty-minute Christmas carol sing. Then silence falls as the congregation prepares for the great Christmas festival.

We stand. The minister, choir, and other worship leaders are assembled at the back of the sanctuary. Suddenly a single a cappella voice pierces the silence, singing "The Proclamation of Christmas." This ancient chant lifts the congregation out of time and places us there in front of the cave, the birthplace of Jesus.

The song ends. Silence. And then, breaking into that silence is the strong voice of the rector crying, "Rejoicing in the birth of the Christ child, let us go forth in peace. Alleluia, Alleluia!" And the people respond together in a loud voice, "In the name of Christ, Amen! Alleluia, Alleluia!" And now the organ together with musical instruments—horns, violins, oboe, marimba—leads the congregation in singing "O Come All Ye Faithful" and "Of the Father's Love Begotten" as the choir and ministers process to their places and clouds of incense rise like prayers to the heavens.

The air is electric with the festive anticipation of the birth of Christ. We hear the Acclamation—"Blessed be God, Father, Son, and Holy Spirit"—and we respond, "And blessed be his kingdom now and forever. Amen." And then the musical instruments lead us

in singing and proclaiming the song Gloria in Excelsis Deo—
"Glory to God in the highest!"

The Christmas Eve service and the services of the twelve days
of Christmas are important because they are festal celebrations of
life. Specifically, they celebrate the birth of Christ; in general, they
celebrate our own life. Life is a precious gift given to us by God the
Creator. The birth of Jesus celebrates this gift and calls us to bring
our own life up into the life of Jesus. The Jesus who was born in
Bethlehem must be born into our own life.

The birth of Christ is the fulfillment of the Advent hope. If a
congregation wishes to experience the birth of Christ as God truly
breaking into their lives, they need to observe Advent. Advent is to
Christmas what Holy Week is to Lent: it prepares the heart to receive Christ and be filled with joy and wonder at the birth of the
Savior of the world.

Epiphany

Epiphany always occurs on January 6 and may be celebrated on
the closest Sunday to the sixth. Originally, it was the date on which
the birth of Christ was celebrated, but the gradual development of
the Cycle of Light placed the birth of Christ on December 25 (re-
placing a pagan festival of the sun) and associated January 6 with the
coming of the Three Wise Men. The days between December 25
and January 6 constitute the Twelve Days of Christmas, each of
which has its own celebration for family worship as well as specific
celebrations for the church.

Epiphany means "manifestation," and this service celebrates the
manifestation of Jesus beyond the borders of Israel to the whole
world. (The Three Wise Men were Gentiles, a symbol of the nations
of the world coming to worship the Christ-child.) Then comes the
season "after Epiphany" which lasts until Ash Wednesday, the beginning of Lent. The Epiphany service and the season afterward always call me to manifest Christ in my own life. How do I let the
light of Christ shine in and through me and witness to others that
Christ is the meaning of life? Will I, in faith and obedience to him
as Savior and Lord of my life, direct others to find the fullness and
meaning of their life in him? In this way, Epiphany calls worshipers
to a spirituality of action, a spirituality of sharing, a spirituality of
witnessing.

The Cycle of Life

The second cycle of the Christian year includes Lent, Holy Week, and Easter and concludes with the day of Pentecost. It is called the Cycle of Life because it deals with the life, death, and return to life of Jesus and calls us into the pattern of dying and rising with him.

I am convinced that this season, which lasts nearly fourteen weeks, lies at the very heart of the Christian faith and is central to both personal and congregational spirituality. Lent and Holy Week anticipate the death of Christ while Easter celebrates the Resurrection. Because the death and resurrection of Christ are not mere intellectual facts, but a vital experience of life itself, I am called to die with Christ and to be raised to newness with him. I am not to be a mere observer of the events; instead, I am to enter into the events, to die and be raised myself. This perspective is the key to vital worship during the Cycle of Life. How can our worship order and organize the experience of the church into the pattern of dying to the old person and rising to the new person in Christ?

Lent

The word "Lent" bears no special meaning except that which has been given to it by the church. In Latin, it simply means "spring," and the church used the word because what it did spiritually to prepare for the death of Christ happened during spring.

In the spiritual pilgrimage through the Christian year, Lent has come to mean preparation. The services during this time order the congregation's spirituality into a readiness for death, not only the death of Christ but also death to our own sin in the death of Christ. Lent is therefore a time of repentance, a time to identify those principalities and powers that control our thoughts and actions, a time to bring our enslavement to sin into the death of Christ, a time to let our own sin and struggles with the powers that rule in our lives be nailed to the cross with Jesus, and a time to let Jesus bury those sins in the tomb, releasing us from them that we may be raised to a newness of life in the resurrection of Christ.

We have all heard stories of how people give up sweets or alcohol or cigarettes during Lent. Indeed, these substances may be powers that control people's lives in a very real way. Lent, however, is also a time for us to wrestle with success and ambition; with our disregard for the poor, the homeless, and those plagued by AIDS;

with our unconcern for abused children and nations at odds with each other; with our inattention to the problem of drugs, divorce, and infidelity. These are not only faraway national and worldwide problems. These problems affect us, and we need to address them. After all, these are problems for which Christ died, and so we need to lift them up into the sacrifice of his death.

We begin to lift our personal problems and the issues of our world into the death of Christ on Ash Wednesday. Ash Wednesday is the beginning of Lent, the beginning of our personal and corporate experience of repentance. I am not nearly as fond of the Lenten services as I am of the Cycle of Light or of Easter services. Appropriately, Lent is sober and penitential, a time to look inward. Even though I am not as fond of this cycle, I am fully aware of its importance and of my own need to enter into a time of spiritual self-examination. The Ash Wednesday service begins just such a time.

The service opens in silence. No one speaks. There is no music, just the hush of complete silence, a sound which in itself calls for inward reflection. The service begins as the minister, dressed in a black robe, walks silently to the front of the worshiping community and leads in a prayer. He calls upon God to "create and make in us new and contrite hearts, that we, worthily lamenting our sins and acknowledging our wretchedness, may obtain of you, the God of all mercy, perfect remission and forgiveness." The minister reads a passage from Scripture like Joel 2:1-2, 12-17 that calls the church to repentance and then preaches a sermon on that Scripture. Next, a call to observe Lent is issued, a call that includes the words, "I invite you, in the name of the church, to the observance of a holy Lent by self-examination and repentance; by prayer, fasting, and self-denial; and by reading and meditating on God's holy Word." After a lengthy litany of penitence and a sober celebration of the Table of the Lord, worshipers are dismissed into a continuing time of repentance.

I am well aware that Lent has not been widely observed beyond the borders of liturgical churches, but this is changing. I now find Lent observed in many nonliturgical churches—Presbyterian, Methodist, Southern Baptist, and Nazarene, to name a few.

When I ask why, the answer I always get is, "Lent is the gospel in motion." One pastor told me, "I take my people through a time of self-examination and repentance so they will experience death and resurrection in their own lives. I want my congregation to die to sin and be raised to newness of life with Christ."

I have always found this pattern true in my own experience. I need an annual time of ordered self-examination, a time when I look at my life, my relationships, my attitudes, and my actions under the searching light of God's Word. Someone might say, "We ought to always live like that." I agree that the pattern of death and resurrection is the pattern of our daily spirituality. We ought to always be sensitive to our sins, repenting, and moving into newness of life.

Yes, repentance and conversion are to be the orientation of my life. But because this is so difficult for me to maintain, I find that the guidance offered to me through the Christian year provides me with an incentive to look more deeply at my own life. Ash Wednesday begins that pilgrimage in me, a journey which is ordered by the worship of the church during the entire season of Lent.

Holy Week

In the Western church, Holy Week concludes Lent whereas in the Eastern church Holy Week is seen as a season in itself. I like to see Holy Week as a distinct season because the worship of that great week leads us step-by-step through the final events of the life of Christ to the very heart of his reason for coming into the world—his death and resurrection.

It surprises me that so much of the Protestant world is inattentive to Holy Week. I don't think we prepare for Holy Week or celebrate the Resurrection with the same kind of intensity we celebrate Christmas. This may reflect the secular pattern of making more out of Christmas, and it may relate to the lack of teaching on the meaning of Easter.

In the ancient church, the Easter celebration—or Pasch (Passover), as it was called then and as it is being called once again—centered around the Great Triduum, the three days from Thursday evening through Saturday night. In the worship renewal of the twentieth century, the services conducted on those days have been restored and changed somewhat to contextualize them for the modern world. Those services are the Maundy Thursday service, the Good Friday service(s), and the Great Paschal Vigil of Saturday night.

The purpose of these services is to allow worshipers to feel the death and resurrection, to enter into these great events, and to experience within them our own death to sin and resurrection to life. Therefore, I must enter into each of these services with the sense that

I am re-experiencing the actual events: it is as though I am there. But these events are not to be experienced as mere historical repetitions of an event. Instead, they are our entrance into the saving benefit, the renewing effect of the event, the breaking through of God into our own lives.

If you want to truly experience the meaning of these three days, set them aside for personal prayer and corporate worship, and do little else except basic meal preparation and housecleaning for Easter. This is not a time to party, to go out with friends, to shop, or to vacation. This is a time to pray, fast, meditate, and enter into the death of Christ. Do this and the Resurrection will come alive as you experience it in a new way in your inner self.

The Maundy Thursday service reenacts the events of the evening Jesus was arrested. It begins with a joyous agape feast either in the basement of the church or in various homes. Then the people gather in the sanctuary to hear the new commandment which Jesus gave to his disciples that evening. ("Maundy" from "mandatum" means "command," and refers to John 13:34 where Jesus told us to, "Love one another. As I have loved you, so you must love one another.") In the Maundy Thursday service, the worshipers also experience the washing of the feet (either the entire congregation participates or, in a symbolic action, the pastor washes the feet of several people in full view of the congregation) and celebrate the Lord's Supper which Jesus instituted on that night. Then the church sanctuary is cleared of all signs of life as the Communion table is washed, symbolically preparing a body for death. After the service ends, the church remains open all night for people to pray and watch with Christ just as the disciples did through that night.

I have gone to church to pray in the middle of the night (2:00 a.m.) or early in the morning (4:00 or 5:00 a.m.), and I always find that the tiredness of my body not only on Thursday night but through Friday and Saturday allows me to experience in my own flesh and bones the enervation of the body and spirit of our Lord. From Thursday night to his death at Friday noon, he received no rest, only pain and torment. I sense that my physical deprivation is closely linked to the intensity of my spiritual experience. My physical weakness helps me enter into the death of Jesus with my mind, my emotions, and my body.

On Friday noon, the church assembles again to mark the time (noon until 3:00 p.m.) that Christ hung on the cross. Worshipers hear and meditate on the last words of Jesus. The people then return for the Friday night Service of the Cross, a service that goes back to the early church. Let me describe this most meaningful time of worship.

We gather in silence. The ministers, wearing black, enter the sanctuary and take their seats. We quietly kneel for prayer, giving thanks to God for the death of Christ. We sit to hear the Scripture and to read together a solemn drama, the Passion story from the Gospels. (The Passion story may also be sung by three people.) Afterwards, we prayerfully sing "When I Survey the Wondrous Cross" and then pray for ourselves, for the church, and for the world.

After these acts of worship, we stand for the Service of the Cross. A large wooden cross is carried into the back of the church, and we turn to look at it. The carrier walks with great reverence a third of the way up the aisle and stops while we sing of the cross, praising it as the instrument of our salvation. The carrier slowly moves another third of the distance toward the front, and we sing again. Now the carrier moves to the front of the church and raises the cross high for all to see as we sing again. Our singing is followed by a deafening silence. We then gaze on the cross, that cruel instrument of death. Now we rise to leave our seats and stand reverently in line. One by one we pass by the cross. Some look. Others touch. A few kiss it. One or two may lower themselves prostrate on the floor. Silence prevails. No music. No instruments. Only silence. Some weep softly. The minister concludes with a quiet prayer, and we leave in silence. I am always moved to speechlessness by this service. In it, I am transported into the Holy of Holies, into the very death of Christ. The death that destroyed death. The death that dethroned evil. The death into which I am invited to bring my own sin that it may be brought to death in the death of Jesus.

Saturday is a day of prayer, of meditation, and of fasting in preparation for the Great Paschal Vigil, another modern service of worship renewal that has its roots in the early church. Of all the services of the year, the Great Paschal Vigil is the most crucial. It is the source of all our worship for it is the chief celebration of the death and resurrection of Christ.

The church gathers on Saturday night at 11:00 p.m. (or early Sunday morning, 5:00 a.m.). After more than six weeks of preparation including two days of intense prayer and fasting, we are ready for the Great Feast of the Resurrection. The sanctuary has been bare since Thursday night. We gather in the darkness either outside or in the vestibule of the church for the first part of the service, the lighting of the fire. Each of us holds a candle which will be lighted by the new fire, the fire that will soon light up the darkness and foreshadow the great event of the Resurrection, Christ's bursting forth from the grave into the newness of life.

The fire breaks through the night in a startling way. The minister's voice is heard over the crackling flames: "Sanctify this fire, and grant that in this Paschal feast we may so burn with heavenly desires that, with pure minds, we may attain to the festival of everlasting light." A large central candle called the Paschal Candle is then lighted, and from that candle which represents Jesus Christ each of our candles is lighted.

We then process into the dark sanctuary that gradually becomes illuminated by the bright light of our many candles. As we are led into the sanctuary, the Paschal Candle-bearer stops three times to cry in a loud voice, "The Light of Christ" to which we all respond, "Thanks be to God." As we take our seats, the Paschal Candle is placed in a stand before us. We snuff out our candles, and a singer standing near the Paschal Candle sings the Exsultet, an ancient song of praise giving thanks to God for delivering us out of the clutches of the Evil One. After the Exsultet, a series of prayers ends this the first of four services that comprise the Great Paschal Vigil.

The second act of worship is the Service of the Word. In the ancient church, the vigil lasted all night during which Scriptures were read presenting the Creation, the Fall, God's covenant with Israel, the prophets foretelling the coming of Christ, the role of John the Baptist, the birth, life, and ministry of Christ, and his Second Coming. Today these readings are shortened to a half hour, but a very important half hour of Scripture which summarizes the history of salvation.

The next act of worship is the Baptism. In the early church, new converts who had been preparing for entrance into the church for some time were baptized at sunrise on Easter Sunday, a fitting symbol of their relationship to Christ through the baptism into his death and his resurrection. Today the renewing church baptizes new believers (and infants, depending on the tradition), and in that service all the baptized believers renew their baptismal vows.

Finally, the church is ready for the fourth act of this Great Paschal Vigil, the Resurrection Eucharist (the word means "thanksgiving"). This is the greatest moment for worship in the entire year. The minister steps forward and, in a loud, clear voice, cries, "Christ is risen!" The entire congregation responds enthusiastically, "He is risen indeed!"

In my congregation, we all bring instruments of noise and at the very moment we cry, "He is risen indeed!," we make a joyful noise to the Lord. Then the organ breaks forth, leading us in a sequence of "Alleluias!" as signs of life are brought back into the church (they were all taken out on Maundy Thursday). Numerous flowers are brought in and placed around the Table, the pulpit, and the organ, and any other place where they can be seen; tapestry such as the hangings at the pulpit and the Table are brought in; and then, with voices, horns, and strings blending together, we all sing the glorious hymn "Christ Our Lord Is Risen Today." We then celebrate a joyful Eucharist. During the Eucharist, we sing Resurrection music and gladly receive the bread and wine, the symbols of the resurrected Christ.

I have been asked by many ministers, "What can we do to make Easter more special?" I've told them, "Go back to the services of the early church and modify them to fit your style of worship." I'm convinced, not only by personal experience but also by the testimony of those pastors and worship committees that have adapted these ancient services for the contemporary church, that we have in these ancient services powerful gifts of the Spirit. These ancient services are gifts of worship that can effectively enable us to truly experience the death and the resurrection of Christ; they are gifts of worship in which God touches our lives and gives us the power to be resurrected into the newness of life.

Easter

In our modern world, Easter is here one day and gone the next, but in the ancient world, Easter lasted for seven Sundays, ending with Pentecost Sunday, the day of the coming of the Spirit. During this season, worship celebrated the presence of Christ among his disciples and marked the Ascension as well. We need to follow this example and focus more on the Easter season, emphasizing the Resurrection as they did and paying more attention to Pentecost, the coming of the Spirit.

The Church of the Servant, a Reformed church in Grand

Rapids, Michigan, decided to make Pentecost special by developing an Eastern service, the ancient St. John Chrysostom Liturgy for Pentecost Sunday. This service, while quite different from the Western service, is fitting worship for Pentecost Sunday.

The service begins with an Entrance hymn followed by a series of prayers which give thanks to God for all of his mighty works, including the gift of the Spirit. Before the Scripture reading, the following litany of the Holy Spirit is said:

Minister: By sending down a confusion of languages, the Most High scattered the nations. By distributing the tongues of fire, God calls all people to unity.

People: In harmony we glorify the all-holy Spirit.

Minister: An almighty wind rushing down from the heavens, The Most High trumpets good news over the earth. And those who cast nets to fish in the sea, Now cast your words to fish among people.

People: We worship and glorify the all-holy Spirit.

All: May the Savior who opens the gates of Paradise,
Open our hearts to wisdom and truth.

The Holy Spirit is emphasized throughout the prayers at the Table of the Lord. A plea for the coming of the Holy Spirit is issued several times: "Send your Spirit, Lord, to make a place for you, among and within us. May our receiving of the bread and wine be our receiving of you." The service ends with the words: "The harvest of the Spirit is love, joy, peace, patience, kindness, goodness, faithfulness, gentleness, and self-control. The Spirit is our source of life. Let us therefore walk by the Spirit."

In an age where the work of the Spirit is being experienced in a new way by people of every group and denomination in the Christian church, the Pentecost service should be a special spiritual experience of praising and glorifying the Spirit.

Conclusion

I have discovered how the services of the Christian year order and organize my spiritual pilgrimage into the pattern of the death and resurrection of Christ, the pattern of new life in him. And I have encouraged churches that do not celebrate the services of the church year to do so as a way of celebrating the gospel more fully and, as outlined below, ordering congregational spirituality. Here is a summary of themes around which the corporate spirituality of the church may be ordered.

Season	Gospel Orientation	Spiritual Focus for the Congregation
Advent	The Coming of Christ	Expect God to enter our lives with his transforming power
Christmas	The Birth of Christ	Let Christ be born within
Epiphany	The Manifestation of Christ to the world	Learn to be a witness
Lent	The Preaching and Teaching of Jesus	A time to identify with Christ, to follow him in every aspect of life
Holy Week	The Death and Resurrection	A time of repentance; a time to take our sins to the cross
Easter	The Resurrection	A time to emphasize what it means to be born anew
Pentecost	The Coming of the Holy Spirit	A time to be open to the power of the Spirit

I am firmly convinced that, with these services, the pastor and staff can lead the congregation into a vital experience of faith, into an on-going discipleship ordered around the gospel. Many worshipers have already experienced a new sense of God's active presence and have felt his transforming power in these services of the church year. These services can truly be called signs of wonder: they help us experience the wonder of God who is for us. Our God not only came historically in Jesus to forgive our sins, overcome the Evil One, and set us an example to follow; but our God comes to us now in worship when we gather to celebrate his work of salvation and re-creation.

Bibliography

The most complete resource for the church year is Hoyt L. Hickman, Done E. Saliers, Lawrence H. Stookey, and James F. White, *Handbook of the Christian Year* (Nashville: Abingdon Press, 1986). To understand where the church year came from, read Thomas J. Talley, *The Origins of the Liturgical Year* (New York: Pueblo Publishing Company, 1986). Good explanations of the church year are found in James A. Wilde (ed.), *At That Time: Cycles and Seasons in the Life of a Christian* (Chicago: Liturgy Training Publications, 1985) and Madeleine L'Engle, *The Irrational Season* (San Francisco: Harper & Row, 1977).

9

◇

The Healing Touch of Christ through Sacraments, Ordinances, and Sacred Actions

Worshiping churches acknowledge that Jesus Christ is the only one who makes us holy and that certain signs given to the church symbolize the saving action of Christ.

I SPENT MY ADOLESCENCE in Montgomeryville, Pennsylvania, a little town twenty-four miles west of Philadelphia, the great city of brotherly love. Montgomeryville is a whistlestop along Pike 309, a highway that moves westward into a number of Pennsylvania Dutch towns. At that time, the most visible landmark in Montgomeryville, along with a gas station and a stoplight, was the Montgomeryville Baptist Church, an old church that stood proudly on a small knoll surrounded by a cemetery full of memories. Folks said George Washington once worshiped there in the original log cabin sanctuary, and I believe it.

I lived about fifty yards to the east of the church in an old but stately white clapboard parsonage with my parents, older sister, and younger brother. It was a roomy old place with wood floors, a study, and four bedrooms, a place that still lingers in my memory.

One of my most memorable moments was a conversation between my father and me in the kitchen when I was about twelve. "Robert," my father said, "I want to talk to you about being baptized."

Several months later, I stood in the waters of the baptismal pool inside the Montgomeryville Baptist Church and heard my father say, "Robert, do you renounce the devil and all his works?" "I do,"

I said in all sincerity, but with little knowledge or experience to know what that meant. "I baptize you in the name of the Father, of the Son, and of the Holy Spirit." Under I went and up I came sputtering and coughing, a newly baptized Christian.

Little did I know at that tender age how much my baptism would mean to me at a later date. I have often reflected not only on the meaning of baptism, but also on its significance for me. That was no trivial event, no mere ritual of puberty. It was a life-changing event which I am still seeking to interpret and apply to my life.

Today, modern worship renewal is paying new attention to the sacraments, ordinances, and sacred actions of the church. Contemporary sociologists and educational specialists are enabling us to see these spiritual acts in new ways. We are seeing these acts as rites of passage for spiritual growth and development, and they actually date back to the early church.

The Meaning of Sacraments, Ordinances, and Sacred Acts

I am well aware of the tensions that exist between various Christian groups and denominations, differences that go back four hundred years to the Reformation. I don't want to get into these squabbles because I am firmly convinced there is a common ground where sacramentalists and non-sacramentalists can meet. That common ground is found in the gospel which worship celebrates.

I began to understand the meaning of the sacred actions of the church and what happened at my own baptism when I discovered the meaning of the word "sacrament." I always thought the word was associated with something magical. My idea of a sacrament was an action which the church did to confer grace. I thought the church did the act in God's name and it was done. The naming was the reality, I believed. And whether or not you wanted the grace, you got it. Some people believe this way, but their belief is more a caricature of what the word means and not a fair presentation of what I believe to be the evangelical meaning of "sacrament" or "sacred action."

I found out that the word "sacrament" derives from *sacramentum*, a Latin word made up of *sacra*, meaning "holy," and the suffix *mentum*, meaning "to make." The word, then, means "to make holy." A good word, I thought!

I also discovered that the Latin *sacramentum* was chosen by

Jerome (the church father who translated the Greek Bible into Latin in the fourth century) to translate the Greek word "mystery." I sensed, too, that this was a clue to the early church's understanding of the meaning of *sacramentum.*

So I went to the New Testament and looked up those passages where the word "mystery" is found. To my surprise, I saw the word "sacrament" used in the Latin Bible in some unexpected ways. Below are some of those references. I have used the word "sacrament" instead of "mystery" so you can see for yourself.

The best place to go is Ephesians where Paul uses the word "mystery" a number of times. Consider this: "Surely you have heard about the administration of God's grace that was given to me for you, that is, the *sacrament* made known to me by revelation, as I have already written briefly. In reading this, then, you will be able to understand my insight into the *sacrament* of Christ . . . this *sacrament* is that through the gospel the Gentiles are heirs together with Israel" (Eph. 3:2-6 NIV); "This is a profound *sacrament*—but I am talking about Christ and the church" (Eph. 5:32); "Pray also for me, that whenever I open my mouth, words may be given me so that I will fearlessly make known the *sacrament* of the gospel" (Eph. 6:19).

I was accustomed to hearing the word "sacrament" in connection with baptism, the Eucharist, confirmation, penance, holy orders, marriage, and unction. But here the word "sacrament" is used in connection with Christ, the church, the gospel, and preaching. What was I to make of this?

Tertullian, a church father of the late second century less than one hundred years after the death of John, provided me with a clue to the use of the word "sacrament" in the early church. In the treatise *On Baptism,* he speaks of water as "a worthy vehicle for God's grace." What I understand him to mean is that water is a sign of a divine action. I heard it put this way once by an Episcopal priest in a sermon at a baptism. He said, "Water does not save; only Jesus Christ saves. And this water is a sign of Christ's salvation as water has always been a sign of salvation in the Scriptures: Noah floated to safety in the ark on the waters; Israel passed through the Red Sea and was saved from Pharaoh; Israel passed through the Jordan into the Promised Land."

The point is that Jesus Christ is the sacrament. In other words, Jesus Christ is the only one who can make us holy. I find this to be a thoroughly gospel-oriented or evangelical understanding of "sacrament." It means that the signs which we call the sacraments, ordinances, or sacred actions of the church are all symbols of divine action. These signs are not ends in themselves or objects of faith, but visible, tangible signs through which we experience a special action of God to save us, heal us, and set us aside for a special calling. These signs, then, become for us an encounter with Christ. And, in worship, Christ—with all of his saving, healing, and comforting power—is delivered to us through various signs.

But there is another side to this view of sacred action, and that is this: We must bring faith, openness, expectancy, and intention to the sign. This is the side of the gospel I have enunciated throughout this book, the side that says faith must be brought to worship. We must participate and respond, or worship doesn't happen. In these acts of worship which have been named sacraments, ordinances, and sacred actions, there is no encounter with Christ unless we will it.

I think liturgical, traditional Protestant, creative, and praise and worship tradition churches can, like the early church Fathers, gather around the understanding that these sacred actions point to the work of Christ. But this may require us to do some thinking about the power of symbols to say and to do.

Symbols "Say" and "Do"

I grew up with a sense of the importance of secular symbols. I remember with fondness all those high school assemblies that began with the Pledge of Allegiance. All of us were required to put our hand over our heart as we said the pledge. There was a sense that this symbol of hand over heart really meant something.

I also recall how desperately I wanted to become a Boy Scout and how I couldn't wait to turn twelve so I could join all my friends in this exciting venture. On Friday evenings when the Boy Scouts met on the first floor of the Montgomeryville Baptist Church, I would wander over by the church, peer through the windows, and, with an ache in my heart, watch their meeting. I wanted more than anything else to join in the fun and challenge.

Finally, I turned twelve, and the big moment of my life occurred around a campfire some sixty or seventy yards from the church next to a winding creek where I swam, built dams and bridges, fished, and even caught a muskrat or two. I stood there by the fire with other boys who were joining this great society of adventurous young men, raised my hand, and was sworn into that body. I could now go anywhere in the world and say, "I am a Boy Scout." I could wear the uniform, gain ready access to the Friday night meetings, go on Boy Scout trips, and, if I wanted, work my way to Eagle Scout.

The point is that with the symbolic swearing-in ceremony—I had raised my hand and said the words of the Boy Scout promise—I became a Boy Scout. Significantly, a two-way action occurred here. On the one hand, the symbol carried the promise of entrance into scouting. On the other hand, my eager and conscious decision to become involved matched the meaning of that symbol, so in that encounter I became a Boy Scout.

Like the young Boy Scout, we all trust symbols in our daily lives: we trust what symbols mean and do. They act, they perform, they realize. The symbol may be as simple as a handshake or as complex as a marriage ceremony and the swearing in of a president. We trust these symbols, however simple or complex, and the promises, commitments, vows, and agreements that they represent. Society depends on these agreements. Without them, life would become chaotic and unmanageable.

Paradoxically, while I was always taught to trust secular symbols, I somehow learned—and learned well—that sacred symbols were of little value and that the best approach one could take to a sacred symbol was to be suspicious of it. Due to this kind of thinking on the part of others, very few Christian symbols were allowed in my worship experience. No one questioned the presence of pulpit, Table, and baptismal pool because these were functional, but I can remember serious discussions about the propriety of a cross, textile hangings, or picture of Jesus. "The plainer, the better" was the working principle.

"The plainer, the better" attitude determined my view of various symbols in worship. At that time, I did not understand that these symbols could be understood as pointing to sacred actions through which an encounter with Christ occurred. Instead, I thought of them as empty symbols because I had been taught not to trust Christian symbols. I saw them as symbols of my action, not Christ's action. I came to the waters of baptism to make a public commitment of my faith. I came to the bread and wine to recall Christ in my mind. The fact is I could make a commitment to Christ without water, and I could intellectually recall the death and resurrection of Christ without bread and wine. So why the symbols? Symbols were empty forms or, at best, nice little aids to the memory—visuals around which I could organize and interpret my experience.

What I didn't yet realize, though, was that we really cannot take away the meaning of the symbol. The supernatural, transcendent meaning remains with water, bread, wine, oil, and the laying on of hands no matter what we do. There is an "isness" about a symbol's meaning that remains despite the most agnostic circumstances. What we can do, however, is build around its meaning a fortress of rejection. We can argue for the emptiness of symbols, we can rationalize away all nonverbal communication, and we can laugh and make fun of visual perception, intuition, and poetic imagination. We can do all this, but all we will accomplish is the building of a personal barrier that prevents our heart, our mind, our will, our soul, our inner person from being open to the action of the symbol. The action is still there, so the significance is still there. Hide it, cover it, bury it, deny it—but it won't go away. All we have done is denied ourselves the benefit of an encounter with Christ which would mold us into his image.

Because Christian symbols open us to transcendence, they have the power to lift us out of the dislocation we often feel in life. They can relocate our disjointed lives into the life of the one who brings order out of chaos and gives us peace. This is the work of the Holy Spirit in conjunction with the symbols, a work which is currently recognized by the charismatics even though the liturgical church has done the work of preserving and handing down the Christian symbols.

Sacraments, Ordinances, and Sacred Actions

I am well aware that distinctions have been made by the church through the centuries regarding the various sacraments, ordinances, and sacred acts of the church. One convenient and widely accepted practice is to distinguish between those sacred actions that are dominical (ordered by Christ himself), those which are ecclesial (determined by the historical church), and those which can be called sacramentals or, more broadly, are viewed as sacred actions which are neither dominical or ecclesial.

What we want to ask as we look at these various groupings of Christian actions is this: What do these actions reveal? At the same time we are asking this question, we need to inquire into the way we handle the sacred action. Do we perform this sacred action in such a way that it contributes to the spiritual health of the participant and to the glory of God?

Dominical Sacred Actions

The two most widely accepted sacred actions of the church are baptism and the supper of the Lord. To my knowledge, every denomination in the world except the Quakers and the Salvation Army practices these actions. While some call these actions "sacraments," others prefer to use the word "ordinance" (ordered by the Lord himself). Regardless of the name used, renewing churches see these actions as vital to worship.

Recently, I was present at the Evangelical Free Church in Fullerton, California, where Chuck Swindoll is pastor. On that Sunday evening, six converts were baptized. What impressed me most about this baptism was the storytelling that occurred before each act of baptism. As the candidates stood in the water, each spoke of life before finding Christ, of how they were found by Christ, and of their new life in Christ.

I was reminded of baptism in the early church (the model for renewed baptism). Before baptism, each candidate renounced the devil. The minister would say, "Do you renounce the devil and all his works," and the candidate would answer, "I do." Then, to symbolize the renunciation, the candidate would spit—literally spit—in the direction of the west, the symbolic domain of Satan. I've always thought of that as a good way to end a relationship.

The early church's understanding of baptism was that it represented the end of one relationship and the beginning of another. As I listened to the testimonials of these candidates at the Evangelical Free Church of Fullerton, I was reminded of the reason baptism belongs in worship. Worship celebrates the victory of Christ over evil, and baptism is a real-life act of relocating one's life from a surrendering to the power of evil to a surrendering to the power of the Spirit. The chief symbol of that action is the rite of renunciation, the spit in the face of the devil.

The symbols at the Table of the Lord are also inextricably bound to the meaning of worship as a celebration of the victory of

Christ over evil and of the application of that victory to our own lives. In my workshops, I celebrate the Table of the Lord using the earliest known prayer of thanksgiving, a text that can be traced back to the middle of the second century and written down by Hippolytus in A.D. 215. In that text, the minister gives thanks to God for the work of Christ. Referring to the works of Christ, the prayer explains that he died "to shatter the chains of the Evil One, to trample underfoot the powers of hell." I love those powerfully descriptive words not only because they describe what Christ did at the Cross, but because they proclaim what Christ does for us now at Table worship. I find that the power of evil is always knocking at my door and that I open that door more often than I wish. I need to have the chains that bind me "shattered"; I need to have that negative power in my life "trampled underfoot." And that is precisely what happens for me at the Table when I am fully open to the way the Spirit applies the work of Christ to me.

There is another benefit I receive at the Table which I need on a regular basis. That benefit is also expressed well in the early church text: the Holy Spirit is asked to come upon all those who worship at the Table, "filling them with the Holy Spirit and confirming their faith in the truth." I'm particularly moved by these words because I, personally, am confirmed again and again in my faith at the Table of the Lord. I have sought confirmation of the Christian faith in my life through both knowledge (evidence that demands a verdict) and experience (I know he lives because he lives in my heart), but nothing has brought me to a deeper conviction of the truth of the Christian faith than the work of the Holy Spirit who confirms the truth of Christ for me at the Table of the Lord.

I am convinced that worshiping churches must recover the Table of the Lord because in this sacred action we are set free of sin, healed in mind, body, and soul, and confirmed in the faith.

Ecclesial Sacred Actions

Space does not permit me to speak to all the ecclesial sacred actions—confirmation, marriage, funerals, the laying on of hands for healing, ordination, or the rite of reconciliation. Let me simply say that a considerable amount of renewal has occurred through each of these actions. The motivating concern to be faithful to the biblical and historical tradition has been balanced by a pastoral concern for the contemporary situation. I will illustrate these changes in one area, the laying on of hands for healing.

About eighteen years ago, one of my former students who was a pastor in a Presbyterian church fell ill with cancer. He believed in the contemporary validity of James 5:14 (NIV)—"Is any one of you sick? He should call the elders of the church to pray over him and anoint him with oil in the name of the Lord." He therefore asked the elders of the church he pastored to anoint him with oil and pray for his healing.

The elders, although believers, were skeptical of such an action, fearing or perhaps not believing in the power of the Holy Spirit. After much discussion and deliberation, they refused to pray over their own pastor who was desperately concerned about his own physical condition and the possibility of impending death. The pastor, shaken by his elders' doubt over the validity of prayer for healing, sought prayer from a fellow pastor who ministered to him in his need. That pastor is still living today and ministering happily in another church.

I tell this story to illustrate how far most Protestants have come in less than twenty years regarding the practice of the laying on of hands for healing. In almost every denomination in the world, the biblical practice of the laying on of hands has made a remarkable recovery. My own experience confirms that people are longing for the touch of the Spirit and his healing in their lives. A pastor who has not offered the laying on of hands for healing should quietly and prayerfully do so.

This past year, I sensed that I should offer the laying on of hands with prayer for healing in my workshops on worship. In September I was in Lodi, California, doing a workshop for a group of Baptists, none of whom had ever experienced the laying on of hands. "This is God's work, not mine," I said. "I'll be on the left side of the church. If you wish to receive the anointing of oil with the laying on of hands, please step in front of me after you have received the bread and wine."

I looked at the people. Seeing neither positive nor negative signs, I continued, "Identify a need you have in your life—it might be relational, financial, emotional, or physical. God knows your need; I don't need to. When you come, I will anoint your forehead with oil, doing the sign of the Cross in the name of the Father, the Son, and the Holy Spirit."

I looked again for a reaction and, seeing none, I went on: "And then I will clasp my hands around your head saying, 'May the Holy Spirit bring healing into your life—mind, body, and soul—and may you be filled with the presence of Jesus Christ.'"

Frankly, I didn't expect anyone to come—and I was completely shocked when nearly half of those in attendance came. For the first time in their life, they received the anointing of oil with prayer for healing. It was obvious to me that many of those who came for prayer came out of a real need and were visibly moved by the event.

We live in a time when many people are experiencing a real and significant dislocation in their lives, and the church is rediscovering the tools given to it by the Spirit to offer healing and guidance. This kind of worship brings people back to worship because it ministers to their needs and provides opportunities for God to touch them with his transforming power.

Sacred Actions

Among other sacred actions which are very important for the spiritual life of the worshiping community are the agape feast, a footwashing service, and, what I'll talk about here, a solemn assembly.

The solemn assembly is rooted in the Old Testament. It occurred at a time of moral and spiritual decline when the people of Israel were assembled together for repentance and renewal. The solemn assembly is being restored today, especially in the Southern Baptist Convention, as a sign of worship renewal. Recently a solemn assembly was held in the Midway Road Baptist Church in Dallas, Texas. I flew there to share this event with them.

Before my trip, the term "solemn assembly" was little more than two words for me. I had read those words and heard them in the reading of Scripture in church, but I had never sat down with anyone who said, "This is a solemn assembly. Here is what happens, and this is the way to do it." Now it was a Sunday and here I was on my way to a continuation of a solemn assembly that had started the day before. I made my way up to the front and sat in the second pew to the left. As I sat, the people to my right turned, looked at me, and smiled a warm welcome.

When the singing had ended, Pastor Glenn Meredith, a handsome young man in his thirties, stepped to the pulpit and quietly said, "I want to give you an opportunity to share what God did for you in yesterday's solemn assembly." A moment of quietness prevailed, a quietness that was charged with energy and a feeling of God's presence. "This is no game," I said to myself, sensing how serious all of the people—including the children—were about what was happening. The silence was soon broken as, one by one, people stood to tell how God had touched their lives. One person said, "I sensed a presence of God in our worship that I have never experienced before."

After many more comments, we sang again. Robert Till, the music minister, led us, and as I sang, I watched him. He had his eyes closed and his head lifted as his lips formed the words quietly, reverently, and with sincere devotion. I was moved by his own worship and by the skillful movement of his arms and hands which communicated like visible voices. He was doing more than leading songs: he was painting a picture of our worship and lifting it to God in praise and wonder. I saw God on his throne and, through Robert's hands, I experienced God's holy otherness, God's transcendence, and the mystery of God's being, a being of love, mercy, and forgiveness. Robert's hands took my feeble praise and gave it flight into the very face of God, and I stood with the angels, archangels, the cherubim, the seraphim, and the whole company of heaven, crying, shouting, and proclaiming the wonder and mystery of God.

After our singing, Pastor Meredith said, "I sense a spirit that no one has orchestrated—a sense of awe and reverential fear. But I believe we are involved in a beginning, not an ending, so we must ask, 'what is God saying to the church?'" Once again the people stood and spoke. One person said, "I feel as though God is purifying our hearts to make us holy as he is holy." Another stood to say, "I feel like I'm a member of the New Testament Church and I'm participating in Pentecost. It makes me want to examine the early church and learn how we can be like them."

After more comments, we sang a little more. Then Pastor Meredith admonished the congregation: "If there is an area of your life not right with God, I want to give you the opportunity to confess it and let God break through the silence you feel in your life. Perhaps you have to deal with your possessions, with a relationship, with an attitude toward someone who has wronged you, with rebellion against your parents, with a sin committed in the past, with someone you have offended, with a critical spirit toward other people. Whatever they may be, I invite you to come to the front and deal with the issues in your life."

Silence prevailed for several minutes, and then a woman in the choir slowly made her way to the front of the church where she quietly knelt on the steps. Soon another woman stood and quickly walked to her side where she knelt beside her and wrapped her arm around her waist. A man behind me walked to the front. When his wife—a member of the choir—saw him, she rushed with swift, determined movements to him and threw herself into his arms as together they dropped to the floor, heads buried in each other's shoulders and weeping softly. Soon the entire front of the church was filled with people who had come to meet God. In quiet prayer for nearly an hour, these people came, bringing their struggles, their failures, their dislocations in life, their burdens, and their sins to be met in worship by the God who forgives, cleanses, reconciles, and restores.

Here was authentic worship in action: people sensed this or that need and, through the surrender of self to God, experienced God's transforming power. The worship service had allowed God to become very present to people who often sense his absence, an absence which many of us feel in the very depth of our being and which makes us long for the presence of God in our lives in some real way. Pastor Meredith spoke again. "If any of you wish to share what God has been doing in your life this morning, please feel free."

As I waited to hear the first response, I thought about how God works in worship. I recalled how worship celebrates the God of history, the God who broke into history to set his people free in the Exodus-event and again in the event of Jesus his son. Jesus lived in the time and space that we know, and he experienced our life and dethroned the powers of evil that constantly seek to dislocate us.

And then I thought about how often we treat the action of God in history as a past event to be memorialized and how dead that kind of worship is. I realized how, here in this church and in other renewing churches, the God who broke into history in Jesus Christ was meeting real present and urgent needs. I felt that the God who came into history two thousand years ago was present now in the worship by the power of the Spirit. I knew in my spirit that the God who comes to us when our marriages are falling apart, when we experience the loss of someone we love, when life is full of stress, when we have lost our job or direction in life, when we have fallen out of relationships with God, with spouse, or with neighbor—that very God was here. When we are dealing with these or other dislocations of life, God meets us in our worship to touch us, to heal us, and to make us whole. Because I sensed that this kind of encounter was happening among these people, I anxiously awaited their response to Pastor Meredith's invitation to share.

A number of people went forward to speak of ways in which the God who breaks into history had broken into their lives. As they spoke, I thought about how we are free to bring to God, the Lord and Creator of the universe, the circumstances of our lives—those things that push us to the very edge and nearly bring us to the breaking point. And then I thought of how the Spirit of God meets us, draws our death into the death of Christ, and raises us to newness of life. And we respond, as these people were, with praise and thanksgiving.

One very moving instance occurred when a member of the pastoral staff stepped forward. "God is speaking to me about my relationship with my wife," he said slowly. "I'm a man preoccupied with my work, and I don't pay proper attention to my wife. I'm too often irritable and cross with her, and I don't show her the kind of love she deserves. I need your prayers and support that God will make me the kind of husband I ought to be." Almost as soon as these words were out of his mouth, Pastor Meredith was at his side.

"You know the devil doesn't want families to stay together. He wants to disrupt marriages and break up families. I think we ought to pray for protection for our marriages and families. I want all the married people in this congregation to stand together. If you are with your spouse, find your spouse and stand together. I'm going to pray for you."

I watched as men and women left the choir to stand with their spouse. The air was charged with emotion as couples met and embraced. Some of them clung together as though to defy the very power of evil that would tear them apart and destroy their relationship.

The prayer that Pastor Meredith offered was certainly one of the most passionate, eloquent, and evocative prayers I have ever heard. In a firm and authoritative voice, he bound the powers of evil against marriage, he sent them to hell where they belong, and he covered the couples with the protecting and reconciling blood of Jesus. Pastor Meredith claimed Christ's victory over the powers of evil, those forces that continually seek to bring marriage to ruin and families to disarray.

I was moved to hear in this Southern Baptist church the proclamation which lies at the very heart of worship—the cry, the shout, the acclamation that Jesus Christ is victor over sin and death. To him belongs marriage, families, people, lives, work, play, and everything under the sun. The power of evil, sin, death, chaos; the shattered lives, broken hearts, disrupted agendas; the greed, hate, murder, lust, envy, and destructiveness in the world—these will not have the last word. The last and ultimate word to echo through the world and be shouted from the heavens is, "THE UNIVERSE IS HIS! HE IS LORD!"

What we do in worship proclaims this message in powerful, God-given language and symbol to those who bring their brokenness to the God who can heal all hurts and restore all lives. This is exactly what was happening at Midway Baptist Church, and it is precisely what can happen in our worship week by week as God meets us in the midst of our fractured existence and moves us toward wholeness. The symbolic action and language of the solemn assembly is just one kind of special service that, through the sacred actions of the church, communicates this saving and healing presence of God, this presence of God in our lives to heal us and bring us to spiritual health.

Conclusion

I have attempted to show how God works to renew our worship not only through verbal means, but also through visible, tangible signs. For this reason, renewing churches are recovering once again the power of symbol and the language of intuition and the senses. God wants to reach the whole person, not just our mind. Similarly, the church that really cares about a ministry to the whole person is a church that will endeavor to meet the needs of the entire person by recovering the communication of the gospel through the signs and symbols of the sacraments, ordinances, and sacred actions of the church.

Bibliography

For an introduction to the sacraments, see Louis Weil, *Sacraments and Liturgy: The Outward Signs* (Oxford: Basic Blackwell Publishers Limited, 1983); James F. White, *Sacraments As God's Self-Giving: Sacramental Faith and Practice* (Nashville: Abingdon, 1983); and William A. Willimon, *Word, Water, Wine, and Bread* (Valley Forge: Judson Press, 1980). For more specific study on the Eucharist, I suggest Robert Fabing, S.J., *The Eucharist of Jesus* (Phoenix: North American Liturgy Resources, 1986); Frank C. Senn, *New Eucharistic Prayers* (New York: Paulist Press, 1987); Kenneth Stevenson, *Eucharist and Offering* (New York: Pueblo Publishing Company, 1986); and Dennis C. Smolokski, S.J., *Eucharistia: A Study of the Eucharistic Prayer* (New York: Paulist Press, 1982).

10

---◇---

Empowering Evangelism, Education, Spirituality, and Social Action through Worship

The worshiping church knows that good worship affects the entire life and ministry of the church and extends to all the activities in which the people of God are involved.

For the last several years, I have been doing workshops on the relationship of worship to evangelism, education, spirituality, and social action. These workshops originated in two experiences which prompted me to begin to think and write about these areas of concern.

The first was a request by St. Mark's Episcopal Church in Philadelphia to conduct a weekend conference on evangelism. I accepted the invitation not knowing what I would say, but knowing if I made the commitment, I would be forced to think more deeply about the meaning and approach to evangelism for Episcopal Christians.

As I thought about my forthcoming time with the people of St. Mark's, I remembered a comment made by an evangelical leader to whom I had given The Book of Common Prayer. After he had read it—or at least read the major liturgies—he came back to me and said, "Why, there's more gospel in that prayer book than you'll find in a Baptist church in a month of Sundays!" He was not putting down the Baptist church, being a Southern Baptist himself, but he was expressing a simple fact: the liturgy of the Episcopal Church, like the liturgies of all the historic churches, is full of gospel.

The gospel is in the prayers, in the Scriptures, in the baptismal service, in the services of the church year, and especially in the prayer of thanksgiving prayed at the Table of the Lord. Here was my first clue to what I later came to understand: worship is the gospel in motion. I discovered that the gospel cannot be proclaimed or acted out in worship without touching on matters pertaining to evangelism, education, spirituality, and social action.

But it was another instance that gave me the context in which I could not just talk about the relationship between worship and evangelism, education, spirituality, and social action. This second experience showed me a way that a church could order and organize the impact of worship in these areas of ministry.

Father Bob Moran, a Catholic priest and chaplain from the Massachusetts Institute of Technology, had come to Wheaton Graduate School to study evangelicalism for a year. Father Moran and I became good friends and often ate together, giving us the opportunity to share our faith and our concerns for the church.

It was during these discussions that I first learned about the Rites of Christian Initiation of Adults (RCIA). The RCIA is essentially an evangelism and renewal ministry originally developed by the second and third century church and recently restored and adapted for the contemporary world. My goal here is to show how this ancient church model can be adapted to the work of today's local church in evangelism, education, spirituality, and social action.

The Ancient Catechumenate

The ancient Catechumenate was originally developed within the church to lead converting and growing Christians, step-by-step, into church membership. These steps of Christian initiation, which pertain to evangelism, education (formation), spirituality, and social action, all flow out of and back into the worship of the church. In the early church, there were seven sequential steps made by converting and growing Christians. Four steps were given to formation, and three were passage rites that effectively moved people from one stage to another. These rites were meaningful acts of worship characterized by symbolic actions that attested to the internal changes taking place in the believer. The seven steps are:

Inquiry
Rite of Welcome
Catechumenate

Rite of Election
Purification and Enlightenment
Rite of Initiation
Mystagogue

At the first of these steps, the Inquiry, the gospel was presented and the inquirers were evangelized. Inquirers then passed through the Rite of Welcome which gave them the status of catechumens within the church. During this three-year period of time, the catechumens were educated and formed by the gospel as it was preached and practiced in worship. During the Catechumenate, almost another three years in length, the candidate was to improve not only in knowledge, but especially in character. Having passed through this stage, the catechumen moved into the Rite of Election. In this rite, also called the enrollment of names, the catechumen's name would be written in the book of life, an act which expressed his/her willingness to follow Christ in baptism. Now the converting person entered the stage of Purification and Enlightenment, a stage which emphasized the nature of the Christian life as a struggle against the principalities and powers of this age. The next step in the process was the act of baptism or Initiation into the church, an act which happened on Easter morning after the all-night vigil. Finally, the growing Christian spent some time in the final stage, called Mystagogue, a stage which incorporated him/her into the life of the church, taught the mystery of the Eucharist, and challenged the newly baptized Christian to be active in social concern.

These stages in the early church were scheduled according to the Christian year. Lent, Holy Week, and Easter were especially important. During that season the candidate prepared for baptism and was then incorporated into the life of the church.

A Modern Adaptation of the Ancient Catechumenate

As knowledge of this ancient form of spiritual development has spread in the last several decades, churches all over the world have adapted the ancient Catechumenate to their own situation. In this chapter, I am proposing that the adaptation of the ancient Catechumenate can serve a local church on two levels: first, as a means of evangelism and the discipling of a new convert into a deeper experience of the Christian faith; and, second, as a means of renewing the faith of a select group of believers already in the church who desire to enter into a deeper relationship with Christ and the church. In each case, worship is the empowering agent of evangelism, education, spirituality, and social action.

The Structure

One of the most important contributions of the ancient Catechumenate to the life of the church is its structure. The Catechumenate enables the church to pay attention to the way worship may empower evangelism, education, spirituality, and social action. While all these concerns need to be before the church at all times, we need to lift each of them up during a specific time of the year, paying attention to a particular area at a particular time. The cycle of the Christian year provides an excellent context for addressing these vital church concerns. Here is a suggested structure:

Season of the Christian Year	The Ancient Catechumenate	Emphasis of the Contemporary Adaptation
After Pentecost (June-November)	Inquiry	Evangelism
First Sunday of Advent	Rite of Welcome	Adaptation of the Rite of Welcome
Advent-Christmas- the Epiphany (Dec., Jan., Feb.)	Catechumenate	Intense period of education into faith
First Sunday of Lent	Rite of Election	Adaptation of the Rite of Election
Lent (6½ weeks before Easter— March, April)	Period of Purification and Enlightenment	Intense Period of Spiritual Formation
Easter Sunday	Rite of Initiation (Baptism)	Baptism of new converts and re- affirmation of baptism by the renewing group—

		and the entire congregation
Easter Season (April–May)	Mystagogue	Intense emphasis on involvement in the church and in social action

In order to communicate how this ancient Catechumenate may be adapted for the modern church, I will comment on each of the seven steps and make some suggestions on what each step might look like in a contemporary church.

Inquiry: A Time for Evangelism

In the early church, the Inquiry was a time to present and discuss the claims of the gospel. This time especially focused on the cost of discipleship: "take up your cross and follow after me." This was an important theme in the second century because the church wanted its people to make a lifelong commitment to the Christian faith over against the pagan world in which they found themselves.

The Inquiry served as something of a clearinghouse: it weeded out those persons presenting themselves to the church for the wrong reasons. The early church did not seem obsessed with numbers and bigness, but instead was concerned about the level of a person's commitment to personal and corporate growth in the faith. For this reason, inquirers were presented with a "life-style gospel" rather than a merely intellectual gospel which they could accept in their minds without having it affect the way they lived in the world.

Today a local church may consider setting up an organization of lay ministers who are called to present the gospel to those who wish to inquire more deeply about the faith. Consider the following scenario:

In the local church, those persons who have the gift of evangelism are identified and commissioned as evangelists on Pentecost Sunday. Between Pentecost Sunday and the first Sunday of Advent, they make a special effort to reach a neighbor, a friend, a fellow worker, or a stranger with the gospel either through personal contact or formal home or business discussions. The people they have reached who show an interest in the gospel are brought to the "ministers of inquiry" who share the gospel with them more deeply. These ministers invite them to commit to Christ as Lord and Savior and to prepare for baptism (or reaffirmation of baptismal vows) by joining the journey toward baptism on Easter Sunday. Each of these newly converting persons is then given a sponsor who has as his/her responsibility the discipling of the new Christian through the remaining six steps of the spiritual journey process. This first group may be called the "converting persons."

A second group of persons from the congregation may also choose to journey through these stages for a different purpose. They may want to deepen their personal faith and commitment to Christ and wrestle more intentionally against the forces of evil with which they struggle. A leader may be assigned to the group as a whole, or each of these persons may be assigned a sponsor who will provide personal discipleship through the stages of spiritual development. It is important for a local church to encourage the formation of this second group called "renewing persons." The steps they take between Advent and Pentecost can have a powerful effect on the life of the entire congregation, especially if a new group cycles through each year.

Now that the two groups have been formed, it is time for the first passage rite, the Rite of Welcome.

Rite of Welcome

In the early church, the Rite of Welcome was conducted in worship to recognize the converting persons and welcome them into the church. This welcome was characterized by several symbolic actions. Most notable of these was the Rite of Renunciation (a renunciation of all other gods and forms of worship as a sign of coming to Jesus, similar to the marriage vows "forsaking all others and clinging to thee alone"); the Rite of Signation (the sign of the Cross is done on the forehead to indicate that this person belongs to Christ); and the Rite of Entrance (the converting person takes his or her seat among the faithful as a symbol of becoming a part of the worshiping church).

These three rites of entrance are relevant today and may be appropriately celebrated on the first Sunday of Advent. A local church should give some careful thought as to the kinds of renunciation a person coming into the faith might make. What are the powers against which a converting person struggles, and how should a new Christian deal with these powers? What kind of commitment should a converting person make to be strong in the struggle against the principalities and powers of this age?

Since the battle against the powers is a lifelong struggle and not a one-time matter, it appears that the Rite of Renunciation seems equally applicable to the renewing group. This group of committed Christians may discuss the powers with which they continue to struggle and then also renounce the powers of evil. Perhaps a different set of prayers would accompany the rite of renunciation for the two groups in order to indicate the particular commitments of the converting group over against those of the renewing group.

Both groups can participate in the Rite of Signation as well as the Rite of Entrance. Again, the words that are spoken with each of these acts would distinguish the different purposes of the converting group and the renewing group.

The Catechumenate: A Time to Emphasize Education

In the early church, the Catechumenate extended over a three-year period. During that time, the converting person attended worship but only the Service of the Word because no one was allowed to receive the bread and wine until after baptism. The Catechumenate was designated especially for character formation and the learning of the Christian faith.

Today, this period for education may extend from Advent to the beginning of Lent, a span of time ranging up to fourteen weeks. While this is not a particularly long time, it is sufficient to deal with the basic content of the Christian faith for converting persons and with an issue or two for the renewing group.

There are several ways this time of education may be used meaningfully for each group. A special class time may be developed for the converting persons to lead them in a study of the Gospel of John or in an introduction to the Sermon on the Mount, the Lord's Prayer, and the Apostles' Creed (favorite topics of the early church). For the renewing persons, a special time of study may center around a book of the Bible or a biblical theme that stresses the relationship between God's Word and a life lived with constant attention to being under its authority. The curriculum chosen for both groups should address the particular spiritual needs of each group, so that an introduction to the faith will be accomplished for the converting persons and a deepening of faith will occur for the renewing persons.

Another way of handling this period of education so that it will be especially tied into worship is to have both the converting group and the renewing group study the texts of Scripture used in worship. The groups should, however, continue as two separate entities so that each will retain its distinct purpose.

In the last few decades, several organizations have developed church school curriculum around the lectionary readings for each Sunday. For example, Living the Good News in Denver, Colorado, has developed an extensive curriculum for the various age groups in the church based on the Scriptures read and preached on from Sunday to Sunday. The idea is to read and study the texts with a group of people before coming to worship. Discussing before worship the texts and their meaning for life stimulates a deeper interest in the use of these texts in worship. It also results in a more significant encounter with the texts of Scripture and the claims over one's life which they proclaim.

Both converting groups and renewing groups could profit tremendously from this study of the Sunday text, especially if there were an additional time after worship to discuss both the text and the sermon. Each group would ask different questions and approach the texts differently, seeking from those texts what is appropriate for a converting person and what is appropriate for a renewing person.

Rite of Election

The Rite of Election occurs on the first Sunday of Lent and is the passage rite into the period of purification and enlightenment. Appropriately, this stage falls during Lent and readies the converting persons for baptism and the renewing persons for the reaffirmation of their baptismal vows.

The Rite of Election is characterized by a simple but powerful symbol called the enrollment of names. It works this way: At a designated time in morning worship, the converting persons are called forward. In a few words, the minister proclaims the biblical truth that God has chosen them and called them to a holy life. He then asks them, "Do you choose Christ?" After an affirmative answer, they step before an open book called The Book of Life and, taking up a pen, write their name in the book. This is a powerful symbol of commitment that speaks to all present, but especially to those who sign the book as an act of their own faith. A similar kind of symbol may be developed for renewing persons. Their action may be ordered around a covenant with God for a deeper spiritual life and may be expressed through the signing of another book, The Book of the Covenant.

In either case, a public affirmation of the desire for a relationship with God is made by both the converting group and the renewing group in the context of worship. The action points out once again that worship is the context in which a relationship to God is established, maintained, repaired, and transformed.

The Period of Purification and Enlightenment: A Time to Emphasize Spiritual Growth

In the ancient church, the period of Purification and Enlightenment focused on developing an intensely personal spiritual relationship with Christ, a relationship that meant rejecting the powers of evil and turning toward the Spirit. While this *metanoia* has been occurring gradually from the very beginning of the spiritual pilgrimage, it is faced here in the period of Purification and Enlightenment with greater intensity. The theme of this period in the ancient church was that of Paul in Ephesians 6:12 NIV—"For our struggle is not against flesh and blood, but against the rulers, against the authorities, against the powers of this dark world and against the spiritual forces of evil in the heavenly realms." During the period of purification and enlightenment, this theme was acted on in daily exorcisms.

The theme of spirituality is essentially that of "living" into your baptism. By this I mean you need to bring the powers with which you struggle into the death of Christ that they might be killed and live into the resurrection of Christ in such a way that you might be resurrected to a newness of life, a living in the Spirit.

The worship of Lent can emphasize this struggle in such a way that the issue of spirituality may be meaningfully addressed by both the converting group and the renewing group. Spirituality can be the focus of sermon texts (groups discuss and apply these texts to their lives) or of special classes organized to address specific issues of spirituality.

One important symbolic way of emphasizing a converting person's and the renewing person's struggle with evil is through the anointing of oil with prayer for the special grace of the Holy Spirit to assist him/her in throwing off evil and putting on the Spirit. A weekly anointing of oil, either in the worship service or at a designated time during the week, is an effective way of communicating the role of the Spirit and of the church in assisting the person to grow into spiritual health.

The Rite of Initiation

In the early church, the Rite of Initiation or baptism occurred in the Great Paschal Vigil of Saturday night as the sun rose on the day of Resurrection. Baptism was full of symbols such as the rite of breathing, a symbol of the Holy Spirit given in baptism; the rite of the renunciation of the devil and all his works; tri-immersion into the Father, the Son, and the Holy Spirit; Chrismation which is an anointing of oil to represent the filling of the Spirit; and, for converting persons, the first experience of the Eucharist.

These symbols and others may be used with the converting persons who come for baptism. A reaffirmation of baptismal vows may be done with the renewing group. However, since it is traditional for the entire church to reaffirm baptismal vows at Easter, a special ceremony may be conducted for the renewing group followed by a general reaffirmation of baptism by the rest of the congregation.

Mystagogue: A Time To Emphasize Social Concern

In the ancient church, the fifty days of the Easter season were used to incorporate the newly baptized into the church, to explain the mystery of the Eucharist (thus the term "mystagogue"), and to encourage people to adopt a life of charity and social concern.

Today, the season of Easter may be used in a similar way. It may be a time when the people of the converting group discern which gifts God has given them to serve the body and people in need. The congregation may urge them toward active involvement in the life of the church, particularly toward those who are in need. The same may be done for the renewing group.

Again, the emphasis may emerge in worship through the sermons. Social concern issues might also be addressed in special classes or committees.

Conclusion

The point of this chapter has been to show how worship is the source of Christian evangelism, education, spirituality, and social action. A story in a letter I received from Cathleen Morris of the Celebration Community in Aliquippa, Pennsylvania, points out this vital connection:

> It is access to daily corporate worship which begins to change old patterns of behavior and offer hope. Being in the presence of people who are worshiping softens and transforms the heart; it focuses and disciplines life. One day at the end of morning prayer, someone asked, "Who is that man? I don't recognize him." He had been coming daily for three months, quietly slipping into the back row and listening to the words of life. He had changed so much internally that he did look like a different man.
>
> When he first came, he was drunk and alone. His family had disintegrated and he was sick in soul and body. The Word, both in Scripture and in song, drew him as did the sharing of the peace and the love of people who cared. At first he was silent; next came tears and then requests for prayer. Finally, transformed by what he had heard and seen and touched, he offered thanksgiving for all God had given him—a new family, a sense of peace, and a place to serve.
>
> That was two years ago. He is now on the vestry and the Pastoral and Evangelism council of the parish. When his friends on the street ask what has happened to him, he tells them that he fell in love with God.

Worship is indeed the source of personal change as we who worship find ourselves touched by God's transforming power. Our personal repentance and renewal, however, then lead us to a life of evangelism, Christian education, committed spirituality, and active social concern. Worship has been the catalyst and will continue to be the guide as we go out into the world to be salt and light.

Bibliography

Persons interested in adapting the ancient form of Christian development should first become acquainted with the material of the early church. I suggest Michael Dujarier, *A History of the Catechumenate* and *The Rites of Christian Initiation* (both published by William H. Sadlier, Inc., 1979) as excellent introductions to the Catechumenate in its historical setting. For primary sources, I suggest Edward Yarnold S.J., *The Awe-Inspiring Rites of Initiation: Baptismal Homilies of the Fourth Century* (Middlegreen, Slough: St. Paul Publications, 1971). For insight into contemporary liturgies for the various rites of passage, see *Rite of Christian Initiation of Adults* (Chicago: Liturgy Training Publications, 1988).

For an emphasis on evangelism, I recommend Robert Duggan (ed.), *Conversion and the Catechumenate* (New York: Paulist Press, 1984); Lisa M. Holash, *Evangelization, the Catechumenate and its Ministries* (Dubuque: Wm. C. Brown Company Publishers, 1983); and Robert Webber, *Celebrating Our Faith: Evangelism through Worship* (San Francisco: Harper & Row, 1986).

For an understanding of the relationship between worship and education, see Gwen Kennedy Neville and John H. Westerhoff III, *Learning through Liturgy* (New York: The Seabury Press, 1978) and Gilbert Ostdiek, *Catechesis for Liturgy* (Washington, D.C.: The Pastoral Press, 1986).

For a discussion of the relationship between worship and spirituality, read Kevin W. Irwin, *Liturgy, Prayer, and Spirituality* (New York: Paulist Press, 1984); Shawn Madigan, *Spirituality Rooted in Liturgy* (Washington, D.C.: The Pastoral Press, 1988); and Don E. Saliers, *Worship and Spirituality* (Philadelphia: The Westminster Press, 1984).

For the relationship between worship and social action, read Mark Searle (ed.), *Liturgy and Social Justice* (Collegeville: The Liturgical Press, 1980); Robert Webber and Rodney Clapp, *People of the*

Truth: The Power of the Worshiping Community in the Modern World (San Francisco: Harper & Row, 1988); and Arthur Van Setters (ed.), *Preaching as a Social Act: Theology of Practice* (Nashville: Abingdon Press, 1988).

APPENDIX I

---◇---

Principles for the Future of Convergence Worship

1. Worshiping people are increasingly exposed to traditions of worship other than their own. This experience of the cross-fertilization of worship traditions is expanding the experience of Christian people and stimulating worship to move in new directions.

2. These new directions in worship are more easily acceptable because of the changing world view of the West. Western thought is shifting from a static view of the world to a more open and dynamic conception of reality. In this new world people are more open to the active presence of the supernatural. This presence and power of the Holy Spirit and of Christ in worship is an antidote to the counterfeit supernaturalism of the New Age.

3. The focus of the more supernatural approach to worship has shifted from the unfolding of an idea to the celebration of an event. The pedagogical approach to worship, which is increasingly being called into question, has been shaped by an enlightenment mentality. The new celebrative approach to worship, which is a celebration of the victory of Christ over the powers of evil, is more typical of the worship of the early church.

4. Many churches are becoming increasingly aware that the present practice of worship is often a time of teaching or evangelism. Concerned to have time for true worship, worshiping churches are choosing a time specifically set aside for the act of corporate worship and designating other times to fulfill the churches mandate for teaching, evangelism, and other ministries.

5. Renewing churches recognize that life-changing worship does not stand alone as a thing in itself, but grows out of attention to the rediscovery of a *Christus Victor* gospel, an experience of the church as the body of Christ, the vital relationship of small group accountability, and the identification and release of every member

ministry. These preconditions to a spirit-filled worship reduce passivity and intensify the participatory experience of worship.

6. Renewing worship builds on the ancient principal *lex orandi; lex credendi,est.*—The rule of prayer is the rule of faith. Recognizing that the way a congregation prays shapes the way it believes, renewing churches now give priority to a worship that celebrates Christ, expects divine presence and action, and provides adequate opportunity for individual and corporate responses of praise, worship, and thanksgiving.

7. The shape of this new Christian worship is like that of early Christian worship. It rehearses a relationship to God in four acts or movements in which the people of God *enter* into God's presence, *hear* God's Word, *celebrate* at the table and are *sent forth* into the world. The underlying structure of each of these acts of worship is the experience of divine action and human response.

8. This fourfold shape of participatory worship is being rediscovered by liturgical, traditional Protestant, creative, and praise and worship traditions of worship. Each tradition brings its own particular style and contributions to this fourfold movement of worship. Thus, worship is moving toward a common shape, enriched by the diversities of tradition.

9. Renewing congregations are discovering how the Holy Spirit engenders an encounter with Christ through the arts in worship. The arts are increasingly recognized as the wheels upon which the text of worship moves. The arts lift worship from an enslavement to words and allow the Holy Spirit to encounter the worshiper through sign and symbol.

10. Worshiping churches are paying new attention to the space in which worship occurs. Space communicates. The wrong use of space isolates, alienates, and closes in on the worshiper. The right use of space opens hearts, engages the body, and frees the spirit to worship.

11. Renewing congregations are becoming aware of styles of music from other traditions. The trend to mix music styles in worship drawing from stately hymns, psalm singing, gospel, new hymns, praise choruses, and Taize music enriches worship and enables the worshiping community to experience new levels of spiritual intensity.

12. Renewing worship is becoming increasingly aware of the power of the Spirit to communicate through the use of drama. Wor-

ship itself is a drama, a script in which God and human persons meet as God's relationship to God's people is played out in the drama of divine action and human response. Mini-dramas within the great drama are effective forms of encounter when they serve the text.

13. Worshiping churches are discovering the freeing experience of using the body in worship. Liturgical churches have introduced an artistic dance that serves the text, while charismatic communities have introduced congregational dance, especially dance which accompanies songs of praise and exaltation.

14. Renewing churches are discovering the evangelical nature of the Christian year. Here, in the special services of Advent, Christmas, Epiphany, Lent, Holy Week, Easter, and Pentecost, the church celebrates the major saving events of history. As congregations re-enact these saving deeds, they enter into God's saving action and find healing and newness of life.

15. Worshiping communities are once again discovering how the power of the Holy Spirit is communicated through sign and symbol. Jesus Christ is communicated through the sacred actions of the church to those who receive with open hearts and hands.

16. Renewing congregations are rediscovering the power of symbolism at baptism. As in the early church there is a new awareness of the presence and power of evil in society and the many temptations to surrender to these powers of evil. Baptism now, as then, is a real-life act of relocating one's life from surrendering to the power of evil to surrendering to the power of the Spirit. The chief symbol of that action is the Rite of Renunciation, the spit in the face of the devil.

17. The worshiping church is recovering the presence and power of Christ through the symbols of bread and wine at the table. Rejecting the doctrine of real absence, renewing congregations are opening the doors and windows of worship to a manifested presence of Christ at the table. Here, the Jesus who died to overcome evil and was raised to begin the new creation is present to bring healing and wholeness.

18. Table worship, as in the early church, is breaking with the sober funeral dirge approach of the Lord's Supper and is recovering the celebrative nature of Eucharist—the giving of thanks for the death and resurrection. The celebrative nature of the communion is experienced through new texts of thanksgiving, communion songs

of high praise, resurrection power and exaltation, and is frequently accompanied by the laying on of hands for healing.

19. The ancient practice of the laying on of hands for healing is being rediscovered by renewing churches as a sign of God's healing power present in worship. In this action all those who struggle receive the power of the Spirit and the prayer of the church to effect healing and wholeness in their lives.

20. The worshiping church continually seeks to relate worship to all areas of the church's ministry. Particularly it seeks to understand and effect the relationships between worship and evangelism, education, social action and spiritual formation.

◇

The Basic Pattern of Convergence Worship

Worship that draws on liturgical and historical resources as well as charismatic and contemporary resources will differ from church to church. Churches that are liturgical or traditional will continue to follow the liturgical and traditional pattern but incorporate contemporary elements at appropriate places. Likewise, charismatic or contemporary churches will draw on traditional and liturgical resources and include them at the appropriate place. Below is the basic pattern of convergence worship. Each church will have to experiment with this pattern to find a style and content most suitable to its character.

Acts of Entrance

The Gathering

The gathering happens as God's people come together to worship. It may begin ten or fifteen minutes before the starting time of worship and contain one or more of the following acts:

Informal singing of praise choruses
Formal organ prelude
Instrumental music
Informal greetings
Announcements
Words of welcome
Rehearsal of congregational music
Quiet meditation

Opening Acts of Worship

The opening acts of worship are characterized by a joyful spirit and a narrative quality. They gleefully fulfill the task of bringing the congregation into the presence of God and readying them to hear the Word of God. Because the opening acts are a joyful journey to the Word, instructive elements of worship are inappropriate. The opening acts or worship may include one or more of the following:

Entrance Hymn or Song

Because the entrance into worship is an act of joy, the hymn or song may be accompanied by many musical instruments such as organ, piano, synthesizer, band, trumpets, flutes, and with a procession of the choir(s) with banners and dance.

Greeting

The greeting is a simple word of welcome or biblical greeting such as "The grace of our Lord Jesus Christ be with you." More charismatic churches may engage in the holy shout to the Lord.

Invocation

The invocation is a prayer calling upon God to be present in the worship of the people.

Acts of Praise

In the acts of praise a great variety of songs of praise may occur ranging from ancient acts of praise such as *The Gloria in Excelsis Deo* or canticles such as the *Te Deum* or an anthem, psalm or praise choruses that lead the congregation from the outer court through the inner court to the Holy of Holies. These acts of praise may conclude with a time of singing in the Spirit or singing individual words of praise together.

Confession and Acts of Pardon

Some churches place the confession and pardon in the Entrance, others in the Service of the Word after the prayers. Confessions and acts of pardon may range from written prayers to informal prayer or silent meditation. In some churches the confession and pardon may be incorporated into the praise choruses.

Opening Prayer

The opening prayer brings closure to the Acts of Entrance and is a transition to the Service of the Word. The theme is usually expressed in the opening prayer. In some churches the opening prayer may be the singing in the Spirit as above (Acts of Praise).

Service of the Word

The Service of the Word is the central act of worship. The Acts of Entrance have brought the people to the Word where they will dwell. The character of the acts of worship in the Service of the Word is instructional. The basic structure of the Service of the Word is proclamation and response. God speaks and the people respond. The mood of the Service of the Word shifts from the joy of the Entrance to a more meditative mood.

The Service of the Word will include the following:

Scripture Readings
  The focal point of the Service of the Word is the reading and proclamation of Scripture. Two or three Scripture readings may be read (Old Testament, Epistle, Gospel) interspersed with psalms, canticles, choruses. For example:

Formal	OR	*Informal*
Old Testament Reading		First Reading
Responsorial Psalm		Chorus(es) Response
Epistle		Second Reading
Canticle or Anthem		

  Scripture content may be communicated through reader's theater, drama, storytelling.
Sermon
  A text or the theme of the text is interpreted.
Response to the Word
  The structure of the Service of the Word is proclamation and response. The people now respond to the Word using a variety of possible responses such as:

  Nicene Creed or some other appropriate affirmation of faith drawn from Scripture.

  Discussion and application of the sermon in small groups of four to six people seated near each other.

  Hymn of Response

  Invitation to receive Jesus, to rededicate one's life to the Lord or to come for baptism or church membership.

Prayers of the People

The congregation, having responded to the Word of God, is now ready to present its prayers to God. In some congregations people with special needs or prayer requests will come forward to a kneeling bench. Prayers may be offered in a number of ways such as:

Group Prayer

The people may stand and turn to form small groups of four to six people.

Bidding Prayers (the prayer leader says: "I bid you to pray for . . . and the people offer prayers out loud).

Litany Prayers (a prayer is said and the people respond with a written response or with "Lord, hear our prayer" or other appropriate words).

Pastoral Prayer

The prayers may end with a prayer of confession and forgiveness (unless done in the Acts of Entrance).

Passing of the Peace

The people offer the peace of the Lord to each other as they shake hands or embrace saying "The Peace of the Lord be with you."

Offering/Offertory

Having been reconciled with God and each other, the people now brings gifts of thanksgiving. As the collection of many is taken, the choir may sing an anthem or the congregation may sing a hymn. If the Table of the Lord is to follow, the bread and wine may be brought at this time (unless the Table has been prepared beforehand).

The Service of Thanksgiving

The Service of the Table and/or thanksgiving is by nature a response to the Service of the Word, the central act of worship. In the early church, it was normative to celebrate the Eucharist weekly. (The word "Eucharist" means thanksgiving and in the early church it was called the Great Thanksgiving.) Renewing churches are moving toward the practice of weekly Eucharist. Where it is not yet the custom to celebrate the Eucharist weekly, contemporary worshiping communities sing songs of praise and thanksgiving followed by the Lord's Prayer. The mood of thanksgiving is celebrative not sober. The acts at the Service of the Table include one or more of the following:

Thanks at the Table of the Lord

Preparation of the bread and the cup. The pastor invites the people to lift their hearts in praise to God. In many churches the ancient invitation to thanksgiving has been restored. It is:

> The Lord be with you
> *And also with you*
> Lift up your hearts
> *We lift them up to the Lord*
> Let us give thanks unto our Lord God
> *It is right to give Him thanks and praise*

Preface Prayer

The pastor prays a brief prayer indicating that the earthly community has joined the heavenly community around the throne of God with all the angels and archangels.

Santus (Holy, Holy, Holy)

The congregation now joins the heavenly choir in singing the new song. Formal congregations may sing the ancient *Sanctus*. More informal congregations may sing contemporary versions or the Holy, Holy, Holy.

The pastor prays a prayer of thanksgiving for the bread and the wine.

The pastor says the Words of Institution over the bread and the wine, lifting the bread and cup for all to see.

The pastor says Words of Remembrance such as "This do in remembrance of me" and/or words that recall the passion, the tomb, and the resurrection.

The people may respond with the words of the mystery of faith:

> Christ has died
> Christ is risen
> Christ will come again

The pastor may pray for the Holy Spirit to come down upon the people to gather them into one and to confirm them in the faith.

The pastor invites the people to receive the bread and the cup. The people may come forward to receive at the Table or remain in their seats.

The people sing songs of praise and thanksgiving. Hymns or praise choruses expressing the joy of the resurrection and exhaltation of Christ may be sung.

Elders and other ministers of the church may administer prayer with the anointing of oil and the laying on of hands. The people may come forward to stations of prayer or after receiving the bread and the wine they may remain at the altar rail or step aside to the station of prayer.

The pastor leads in a closing prayer.

Thanks without the Table of the Lord

On those Sundays when the Table of the Lord is not celebrated, the people may give thanks through a prayer of thanksgiving or through hymns or choruses of praise and thanksgiving. This time of thanks may be concluded with the Lord's Prayer if it has not been prayed previously.

The Acts of Dismissal

The Acts of Dismissal bring closure to public worship. The pastor should send the people forth in joyful recognition of their responsible service to the world. The mood is one of joy. The sense is that of going forth. The Acts of Dismissal include one or more of the following:

Announcements
If announcements have not been given in the gathering, they may be given here. As the people go forth they are reminded of the activities of the people of God during the week.

Benediction
The people are blessed with a word from God that empowers them for life in the world.

Dismissal Hymn or Song

The hymn signals going forth. If the Entrance Hymn was accompanied by a procession with music, banners, dance, etc., the Dismissal Hymn should do the same.

Words of Dismissal

These words close the worship and send the people forth. For example:

Go forth into the world to love and serve the Lord. Thanks be to God! Alleluia!, Alleluia!

In some congregations the service ends with clapping to the Lord.

Conclusion

In *Signs of Wonder* I have attempted to reveal what is happening in worshiping churches all over the world. Because this renewal is so vast and because this book has dealt with the phenomena of convergence in a surface way, you may be longing for some more information and help.

This book is the first of a number of resources and tools that are being made available for the local church. Here are several other resources designed with the local church in mind that you will find helpful:

First, *The Worship Diagnostic* (Nashville: Abott-Martyn Press, 1992). This tool has been designed to help a congregation determine its own pattern of worship renewal. It contains an extensive self-evaluation questionnaire, numerous specific suggestions and resources, and details the seven stages a local church passes through as it seeks a worship rooted in the biblical tradition, aware of historical resources, and vital for the contemporary worshiper.

Next, a virtual encyclopedia of worship resources is being made available in *The Topical and Illustrated Encyclopedia of Christian Worship* (Nashville: Abbott-Martyn Press). This seven-volume work will be published consecutively starting in the fall of 1992 through the winter of 1994. The seven volumes are as follows: *Vol. I, Biblical Resources; Vol. II, Historical and Theological Resources; Vol. III, Resources for Sunday Worship and Preaching; Vol. IV, Resources for Music & the Arts; Vol. V, Resources for Services of the Christian Year; Vol. VI, Re-*

sources for Sacraments, Ordinances and Sacred Actions; Vol. VII, Resources for Worship and Related Areas.

In addition, the Institute of Worship Studies (Wheaton, IL) has been founded to be a training school for persons who lead worship and others who desire to learn more about the history, theology, and practice of worship. The courses of IWS are all extension courses which can be taken in the convenience of the home and lead to the Certificate of Worship Studies (CWS). The school opens in September, 1992. For a brochure write Institute of Worship Studies, c/o Star Song Publishing Group, P.O. Box 150009, Nashville, TN 37215.

These and other resources to be published by Abbott-Martyn Press are designed as tools to help the busy pastor and worship leader provide genuine spiritual leadership through an ever-renewing experience of worship.